BASICS
FASHION MANAGEMENT

Clare McTurk and Dimitri Koumbis

Fashion Buying

From Trend Forecasting to Shop Floor

Third Edition

BLOOMSBURY VISUAL ARTS
LONDON · NEW YORK · OXFORD · NEW DELHI · SYDNEY

BLOOMSBURY VISUAL ARTS
Bloomsbury Publishing Plc
50 Bedford Square, London, WC1B 3DP, UK
1385 Broadway, New York, NY 10018, USA
29 Earlsfort Terrace, Dublin 2, Ireland

BLOOMSBURY, BLOOMSBURY VISUAL ARTS and the Diana logo are trademarks of Bloomsbury Publishing Plc

First published in Great Britain by Fairchild Books 2014

This edition published by Bloomsbury Visual Arts 2025

Copyright © Bloomsbury Publishing Plc 2025

Clare McTurk & Dimitri Koumbis have asserted their right under the Copyright, Designs and Patents Act, 1988, to be identified as Authors of this work.

For legal purposes the Acknowledgements on pp.189–190 constitute an extension of this copyright page.

Cover image © Ms Gayle Fenny

All rights reserved. No part of this publication may be reproduced or transmitted in any form or by any means, electronic or mechanical, including photocopying, recording, or any information storage or retrieval system, without prior permission in writing from the publishers.

Bloomsbury Publishing Plc does not have any control over, or responsibility for, any third-party websites referred to or in this book. All internet addresses given in this book were correct at the time of going to press. The author and publisher regret any inconvenience caused if addresses have changed or sites have ceased to exist, but can accept no responsibility for any such changes.

A catalogue record for this book is available from the British Library.

A catalog record for this book is available from the Library of Congress.
Library of Congress Control Number: 2024942539

ISBN: PB: 978-1-3502-8057-1
ePDF: 978-1-3502-8058-8
eBook: 978-1-3502-8059-5

Series: Basics Fashion Management

Typeset by Integra Software Services Pvt. Ltd.
Printed and bound in India

To find out more about our authors and books visit www.bloomsbury.com and sign up for our newsletters.

Figures 0.1–0.2 Seasonless Fashion: the timeless pea coat.
Timeless classics at the heart of sustainable fashion, products that become season free, do not change with seasonal trends, investment pieces that can be sold and worn right through the year, designed with longevity, provide the perfect complement with seasonal items.

Contents

Introduction vii
Chapter Summary viii

1
The Fashion Buyer 1

The fashion retail environment 2
The buyer's relationship with the retail environment 2
Types of retail stores 4
What is a fashion buyer? 10
Buying teams and their working environment 12
Fashion buying approaches and the consumer 17
Product-specific purchasing 24
Case study: The Global Buying Director: Andrew Searson – Adidas 30
Chapter 1 summary 34

2
Sources of Buying Inspiration 37

Buyers and market intelligence 38
Market research 42
Focus on the customer 45
Trend forecasting 49
Buying markets 51
Competition shopping 54
Case study: SEEK Berlin at Berlin Fashion Week: Damien Winpenny, Sales Manager, SEEK Tradeshow 62
Chapter 2 summary 66

3
Suppliers, Sourcing, and Communication 69

The fashion designer–buyer–quality assurance (QA) relationship 70
What is a supply chain? 74
The buyer–supplier relationship 77
Managing the supply base 79
Monitoring supplier performance 80
Sourcing issues 82
Developing product categories and selecting lines 88
Fabric selection 91
Fashion lead times and the fashion buying cycle 92
Fashion buyers and fabric sourcing 93
Selecting and buying garments 98
Case study: The designer and buyer/merchandiser relationship: Stephen Park & Stephanie Stumbaugh discuss their perspectives 99
Chapter 3 summary 107

4
Range and Merchandise Planning 111

What is merchandise planning? 112
The buyer–merchandiser relationship 114
The buyer's instinct vs planning 114
How a buyer's success is judged 115
The merchandise planning process 120
Developing the initial seasonal buying plan 122
Merchandise pricing 125
Risk and range planning 129
Getting the range balance right 132
Selecting and grading the store ranges 133
Product sampling and final range preparation 134
Case study: WhichPLM, Mark Harrop – Expert Fashion Process & Technology Advisor 138
Chapter 4 summary 144

5
Trends in Fashion Buying 147

Consumer connection promotional activities 148
Branding, advertising, and marketing 148
Social media and the AI influencer 150
Visual merchandising 152
Showtelling and pop-up 154
Fashion technology and the digital fashion landscape 156
Corporate social responsibility (CSR) 160
Fashion circularity 165
Intellectual property rights (IPR) 166
Case study: CLO Virtual Fashion Incorporated: Simon J.H. Kim – Global CEO 167
Chapter 5 summary 172

Conclusion 174
Glossary 176
Industry Resources 179
Index 183
Acknowledgements and Picture Credits 189

Introduction

Working in fashion is competitive and exciting, and the fashion buyer's role is one of the most sought-after careers in the fashion industry. The buying role may have a glamorous image with opportunities to travel around the world to choose the latest styles from international showrooms and trading events; however, it is a role that requires a combination of business, analytical, and creative skills. The fashion buyer's main task is to select best-selling lines that will appeal to their target customers and more importantly that will sell out quickly, therefore buyers need to understand the latest trends, colours, and styles of the season. Working closely with a designer and merchandise planner, it is the fashion buyer who ensures that the business is adequately stocked at the right time, with enough best-selling lines to meet the company's planned sales and profit.

Fashion Buying, third edition, will explore what fashion buying entails in terms of the activities, processes, and people involved, all from the perspective of the fashion buyer. The fashion-buying role is globally recognized; however, the role can vary from business to business and brand to brand, ranging from buyers who develop house product for the lower-priced discounters and supermarkets, to those who work for high-end department stores selecting 'Ready to wear' ranges from well-known prestige brands. Each level of buying requires a slightly different approach, and each has its own nuances; but in general, most require the same processes, skills, and understanding with only the product and the customer being the changeable element.

Fashion Buying, third edition, has been divided into the five main areas of buying activity: summary of the buying role; sources of inspiration; suppliers, sourcing and communication; range and merchandise planning; and contemporary trends in fashion buying. The book will focus on real-life fashion buying, that is, mainstream fashion buying – where most jobs and opportunities exist within the business. In *Fashion Buying*, third edition, there is an expansion on many of the topics previously discussed and new case studies have been incorporated to reflect the changing nature of the fashion industry. An introduction to the basic principles of merchandise pricing and costing will give the reader a stronger understanding of how buyers calculate markups and markdowns to help turn a profit.

Figure 0.3 Fashion is in the eye of the beholder.
Gangster and hip-hop style combined with the elegance of faux fur and pearls.

Chapter Summary

Chapter 1

This chapter will focus on the fashion buying retail environment, identifying and discussing the variety of retail environments and the relationships the buyer develops that play a significant role in achieving business success. The intense and varied nature of the buying role is aligned with the inherent need to understand the consumer to drive success. The skills, personality, and attitude needed for successful fashion buying are explored, providing valuable information that will benefit specialist buying professionals wishing to enhance their own career prospects.

Chapter 2

Buying is not only a creative skill but requires business acumen and decision making; fashion buyers must be responsive to an ever-changing fashion landscape and to the needs and wants of the digital consumer. This chapter will focus on the marketplace, trend forecasting, and how buyers work with designers to plan and buy new ranges, often seasons in advance of customers buying them. Timing is essential – buyers must respond to the market analytics and the fast paced retail environment. This chapter will discuss the fashion calendar and the associated trade fairs, exhibitions, conferences, and events that provide sources of inspiration and global trade.

Chapter 3

Chapter 3 will focus on sourcing, selection, and supplier planning, identifying how product is sourced locally, nationally, and internationally, and discussing the changing nature of the fashion supply chain. This chapter will explore how the buyer interacts with the design, marketing, technology, and merchandising departments, which all contribute to producing the right range offer in terms of lines, categories, width, and depth. Strategic sourcing is a key buying activity – buyers have to work within lead-time restrictions and fashion cycles. This chapter reveals the dilemmas faced by today's buyers in final supplier and range selection.

Chapter 4

The development of a digital fashion landscape has enhanced the need to get the right product to market at the right price, in the right place, and at the right time. The fashion market is one of the most unforgiving. To this end, in this chapter we examine how fashion buyers and merchandisers undertake detailed levels of line, product planning, sampling, and costing to ensure that they present the best offer to the consumer.

We look at how merchandise planning increasingly constitutes a large part of the fashion buyer's activities and how the merchandiser works alongside the buyer, enabling them to concentrate on the more creative aspects of the role. Merchandise pricing and key performance indicators (KPIs) used to identify and drive potential profit and risk management are explored.

Chapter 5

Fashion retail is evolving and becoming a very diverse and interactive landscape; with an uncertain future there is a need to provide sustainable solutions to the exponential growth that the fashion industry has seen. In this final chapter, we will examine emerging trends and diverse consumer demands that are developing in the light of global sustainable issues and how fashion is adapting through the use of data and consumer analytics to combat over-consumption and embrace the future of digital fashion and digital fashion consumption. Chapter 5 also looks at various trends in buying, from the change in promotional activities that generate demand for goods to technology that facilitates stronger communication between buyers and retail.

Within each chapter, you'll discover interviews with key fashion professionals, which put the contents of the chapter into context and perspective, offering you unique insights into the business of fashion buying and the challenges facing buyers today. Business case studies demonstrate the activities described, and practical activities are suggested that enable you to work through the ideas explored in each chapter.

The actual fashion buying process represents only one stage along a long and very complex supply chain, which often involves hundreds of individuals. Fashion buying is also an intellectually demanding job, with so many activities to undertake in so short a time – often with a fast-changing market to further complicate matters. Any experienced buyer will tell the reader that simply having a 'passion for fashion' is just not enough. Grit, determination, drive, dedication, and empathy are also needed in equal amounts.

Good luck with your career in fashion buying!

The Fashion Buyer 1

The fashion buyer is a commercial and creative thinker, data savvy, and one step ahead of the competition. Although the role of a fashion buyer is commonly linked with glamour, it requires sharp business acumen, meticulousness, and unwavering determination. Fashion buyers operate in a fiercely competitive environment encompassing various industry sectors, ranging from discounted products to technical sportswear and boutique to luxury brands, and the decisions they make have a direct impact on the success of a collection or brand.

The fashion industry is diverse and complex, with a global work force of more than three million and a global revenue in excess of three trillion. The international high street is diverse and volatile; how buyers operate can differ significantly. A department store buyer may choose from existing branded collections, whereas a buyer for a mid-range, private-label clothing brand must create an entirely original range. Irrespective of the sector, the success of any fashion range depends on the buyer's ability to purchase a unique range of products that generate revenue, entice the consumer, and achieve corporate sustainability goals.

Figure 1.1 Reptilian textures combined with timeless silhouettes for Versace FW23 at the Pacific Design Center in West Hollywood.

The fashion retail environment

The fashion retail environment encompasses a diverse range of entities spanning from the traditional high street multiples to the global online omnichannel retailers. To navigate this fiercely competitive arena, it is crucial to comprehend the inner workings of the fashion retail landscape in order to determine the position of buyers. One of the defining characteristics of the fashion retail environment is its rapid and dynamic nature. Trends emerge and fade quickly, prompting retailers to continuously adapt and introduce new collections to cater to evolving consumer preferences. This rapid turnover of styles has been further accelerated by the rise of social media and online shopping, as consumers are now exposed to a constant stream of fashion inspiration and are eager to stay up to date with the latest trends. However, recently there has been a notable shift in consumer preferences, with an increasing emphasis on sustainability and ethical considerations within the fashion industry. Consumers are now more conscientious of the environmental and social ramifications of fashion, and they actively demand transparency and responsible practices from retailers.

Considering these changing dynamics, fashion buyers play a vital role in navigating the fashion retail environment. They must possess a profound understanding of consumer behaviour, market trends, and business strategies. Trend forecasting and analysis of market data enable buyers to make informed decisions regarding product assortments and inventory management.

The buyer's relationship with the retail environment

The fashion retail sector has changed dramatically over the last 30 years. Technological developments are enabling consumers to connect and purchase fashion products in many new and diverse ways. A comprehension of the retail environment where their range is sold influences the buying decisions made. Understanding the connection that a product has with its core consumer is crucial for fashion buyers in making informed purchasing decisions. They must grasp the relationship between a product and its core consumer to ensure the right merchandise is selected. Development in big data is empowering the buyer to use technology to connect with the retail and the consumer environment. Data harvesting tools and consumer engagement in social media are becoming much more influential to the success of a fashion product.

Communication between the buying teams and the retail environment is important in this relationship and will inform buying decisions that drive sales and achieve higher units per transaction (UPT). It is vital to establish how well the consumer receives products and their reactions to new lines so that the buyer can manage risk and ensure each range and each item achieves its goal, which is to make a profit.

Engagement in the retail environment allows the buyer to see what is really happening in the market; not only will they assess the competition, they will use their research to ensure that seasonal re-buys are based on consumer and market needs. It is important that the buyer has a holistic view of the fashion retail environment, as it can vary from city to city. To understand the retail environment and the competition, buying teams will visit key fashion cities well ahead of the season to preview the next season's range to key retail staff, providing them with information such as colour stories, fit changes, and new brand launches. Retail managers get a top-down view of their products in store visits which give retail staff the opportunity to provide valuable feedback on both the successes and perceived opportunities within the range; this feedback will help to inform buying decisions and mid-season re-buys. Technology and the online retail environment have enabled the buyer to get direct access to consumer feedback on social media, and posts of instant gratification or dissatisfaction about a product can lead to immediate success or devastating failure of a line. Major online players like Fashion Nova offer incentives and collaboration deals to their customers to review their products and share their reviews online, mastering customer to customer marketing and following. Ultimately, the role of the fashion buyer within the retail landscape is instrumental in shaping a successful product offering that satisfies customers and drives business growth. Considering the changing retail dynamics, fashion buyers play a vital role in navigating the fashion retail environment. They must possess a profound understanding of consumer behaviour, market trends, and business strategies. Trend forecasting and analysis of market data enable buyers to make informed decisions regarding product assortments and inventory management.

Figure 1.2 The future of retail. Incorporating digital screens, augmented reality and life size avatars. Here a consumer is using a virtual reality simulator with touchscreen capabilities to shop online.

Types of retail stores

The fashion industry is a commercial, for-profit business like any other, and it begins and ends with the customer. Research into consumer behaviour and spending patterns drives the creation and development of innovative fashion to suit customer needs. Fashion retailers and brands trade in many different formats: department stores, discount outlets, and online platforms are mainstream; however, many retail brands are embracing multi-channel approaches that include social media, shopping apps, and interactive experiences (Figure 1.2). The developments in retail technology allow the buyer to access information on consumer spending habits more than ever; understanding the different retail typologies and interpreting consumer data means that fashion buying predictions can be more accurate and consumer focused. Many fashion retailers are adopting an integrated approach, developing unique customer experiences that promote personal relationships between the consumer and the brand. The retail fashion high street is now a hybrid of physical and digital activity and can be segregated into distinct categories.

Department stores

Mostly found in large urban cities and suburban malls, department stores sell a wide range of goods from high fashion to electronics. Often known as the anchor store of the high street or mall, they add value by offering quality and craftmanship, and are known for their customer experience and service. Department stores cater to a wide demographic, more so than most retail types. Most department stores offer an omni-channel approach with physical stores, online platforms, mobile apps, and social media, providing a seamless transition for customers as they navigate between the different modes during their shopping journey. Using concessionary agreements, department stores can often be the retail gateway for up-and-coming specialty brands. Famous department stores include Selfridges (London), Galeries Lafayette (Paris), Macys (New York), and Ka-Da-We (Berlin).

Specialty retailers

Small-to-large space retailers, which usually form part of a larger shop chain with flagship locations, these retailers may be gender-specific or market exclusively to families (men, women, and children). They trade at various market levels, generally termed low, middle, and high. Specialty retailers support a narrower demographic based on their product and market position. Low-end examples include Old Navy (USA) and Primark (UK); Gap, Monsoon, J. Crew, Kurt Geiger, Whistles, and Zara are typical middle end (internationally); and high-end tend to comprise either locally known or national brands, such as Max Mara, Burberry, and Stella McCartney (UK), or international brands such as Ralph Lauren, Mark Jacobs, and Off-White (USA).

Figures 1.3–1.4 Fashion at work.

Fashion retailers target certain demographics based on their retail typology. A department store, such as Harvey Nichols (above left) offers a wide range of products for a vast consumer base, whereas a specialty store such as Urban Outfitters caters to a niche market, offering a narrower product assortment.

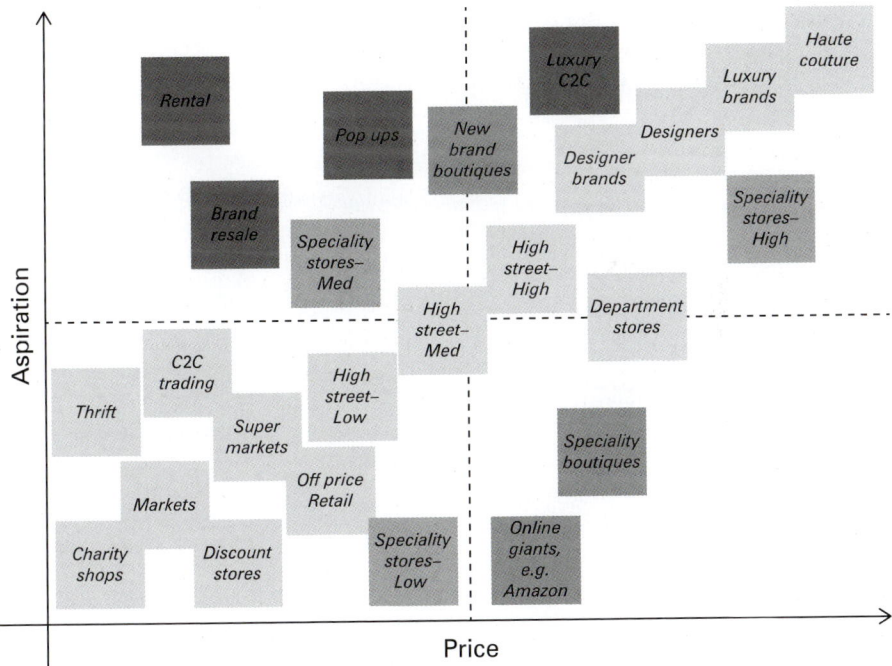

Figure 1.5 The continuum of clothing and fashion.

Fashion is exchanged and marketed at a range of levels across society, from customer to customer, trading to the multimillion-pound marketplace represented by haute couture.

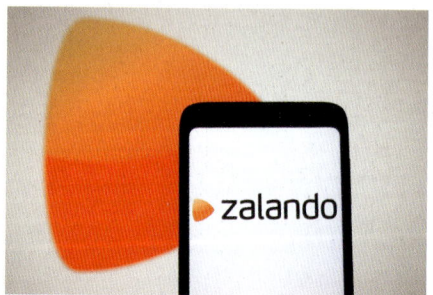

Figures 1.6–1.8 Market levels.
There are so many different types and market levels of fashion retailing, and each targets its own segment of the market, be it a department store such as Macys; a multi-channel, multi-geography distribution store such as Kate Spade; or an e-tailing giant such as Zalando.

Boutiques

Accounting for a large share of the clothing retail sector, boutiques have a huge impact on the clothing retail economy. Often found in smaller towns and suburban areas, boutiques predominantly are independently owned and operated. Due to the COVID-19 pandemic in 2021, in an attempt to survive, boutique owners developed online selling platforms, relying on social media to maintain product loyalty with their valued consumers. Social media platforms such as TikTok and Instagram have revolutionized the selling platforms for boutiques, known for their addictive nature and substantial user engagement; users can produce, view, and distribute 15-second videos captured using mobile devices or webcams. Boutiques offer a narrow range of specialty goods, predominantly other fashion labels (but sometimes private labels or custom designs, too). Their product is typically at a higher price point and selectively restocked, so quantities are often limited. At boutiques, the shop owner usually acts as both the manager, buyer merchandiser, marketing, and creative content lead.

Discount retail and the grey market

These big-box retailers are like department stores, but they typically sell goods at significantly lower price points. They buy in large quantities in an effort to pass their savings on to consumers. A savvy shopper can find end of season high fashion brands and family favourites that have strong market following. Discount operations sell a variety of products from fashion apparel to homeware and beauty products. Well-known discount operations include TK Maxx (UK), Tesco F&F (Europe), and Target (USA).

Supermarkets and hypermarkets

Historically, supermarkets and hypermarkets mainly sold food, but in an endeavour to achieve higher profits and provide a 'one stop' service, many now stock their own clothing brands. This is particularly strong in the United Kingdom and Canadian markets, but it is becoming increasingly popular in the United States. Joe Fresh for Loblaw in Canada, for example, is a private fashion label that has recently branched out into freestanding brick-and-mortar locations in the United States. George at Asda is a national UK brand closely followed by Sainsburys TU and Morrisons Nutmeg. In Europe, the supermarket chain Leclerc sells fashion under the brand Clace, and Walmart retail a number of named and own brand products.

Factory outlets and factory village stores

Factory outlets were originally created on factory sites to sell off faulty or excess stock. Today, many upmarket and mid-market brands sell overstock, faulty items, and exclusively produced lines in these more remote retail locations. The large-scale factory village was originally an American concept, but the idea has quickly spread around the globe and can be found in most major countries (e.g. Bicester Village and Cheshire Oaks, United Kingdom).

Figure 1.9 eBay Fashion Shop & Sell Boutique in Berlin.
Pioneering the term 're-commerce', customer to customer e-tailing has seen significant growth over the last 3 to 5 years particularly in the second-hand market with the development of online trading platforms and applications like Depop, Vestiaire, Vinted, Poshmark, and eBay. Fashion retailers are also tapping into the resale market with the development of re-commerce platforms like ASOS marketplace and the garment collection programmes offered by H&M and Zalando.

Vintage, charity, thrift, and re-commerce

Sustainability issues and the concepts of upcycling have been major drivers in the development of the clothing resale market, along with an increased consumer desire to source unique products. Approximately 9,000 charity shops selling pre-worn clothing operate in the United Kingdom alone, and the numbers are spreading globally as fashionistas shop vintage and thrift to find unique additions to their personal wardrobes. Pioneering thrift in Germany is second-hand and vintage chain Humana with thirty-seven stores in 2022 and they are capitalizing on followers to educate in fashion sustainability and individual fashion style. https://www.humana-second-hand.de/mode/first-class.html

Online pure players, e-tailing, e-commerce, and digital sales

Fashion retail has been transformed by the development of e-tailing, the sale of goods through online platforms offering 24/7 shopping to the consumer from wherever they are based. Retailers can reach out to a plethora of consumer markets across the globe via personal computers, smartphones, and tablets. The digital global fashion trade has allowed online retailers from around the world the ability to tap into new markets. Online giants Shein, Lazada, Poshmark, Wish, and Fashion Nova now compete in the same landscape as BooHoo, Zara, ASOS, and Forever 21. A new entrant in the marketplace trading sphere is Temu, operating in a comparable way to Amazon or AliExpress, offering cheap and readily available fashion brands the opportunity to trade round the world with ease. Temu support their brands through social marketing practices that maximize discounts, emphasize rewards, and support 'refer a friend' incentives. Fashion e-tailing allows for precise product information to be shared with the consumer, including availability, sizing, and delivery times. Retailers can maximize on the influence of consumer-to-consumer reviews. The technology has advanced in so many ways that there are opportunities to engage in virtual fitting rooms and virtual store fronts, and tracking of data will help the retailer to suggest complementary products and replacements when stocks are depleted. Retailers who use digital applications can engage the consumer in personalized ways by storing data of past purchased product and giving loyalty discounts. Fit remains a problem for online shopping and a high percentage of products are returned; however, technological advancements in initiatives that enhance fit like the magic mirrors, https://www.magicmirror.me/Apps/3D-Virtual-Dressing could give us the ability to try on garments virtually in our own homes. Websites like Fit Finder, https://www.fitanalytics.com/fit-finder, and Look Size https://www.looksize.com/ work with retailers to suggest the best fit products. Some retailers are trying to influence the consumer to make better choices when buying online. Many consumers will buy more than one size or colour to have the opportunity to try on at home and return for free, driving up the use of energy and plastics in packaging. Retail giant Inditex and fashion label Zara have recently introduced a return charge in the United Kingdom of £1.95 ($2.39) to return product bought online. Their rationale for this charge is environmental factors, but free returns are still available in store.

Other types of retail outlet

Airports, train stations, hospitals, and large office complexes are now utilizing spare square footage for incorporating different retailer types. Some companies run short-term pop-up shops or home and office selling parties, there really are no boundaries to where fashion can be sold. Additionally, concessions refer to small brands or designers that rent space inside the stores of larger retailers, paying weekly commission (or a contractual amount) on the sales that they have achieved. These offer unique selling points that traditional retail types may not be able to provide. Coal Drops Yard, https://www.coaldropsyard.com/ is a shopping destination in London that has monthly 'Drops' that feature some of the United Kingdom's most up-and-coming designers, providing flash retail opportunities to test new lines and trial a retail space.

National brands vs private labels

Fashion retailers either stock products that they have developed and manufactured for themselves, which are generally uniquely sold in their own business (private label buying), or they may buy ready-designed existing brands from manufacturers and/or design houses (national or international brand buying). Retailers such as department stores often sell a combination of the two.

National (or international) brand buying requires the buyer to select which brand names or designers are to be stocked as well as to select and sub-edit the individual lines to be stocked or bought from each range. Buying branded merchandise requires the buyer to pick those elements of the branded range that best fit their own business and customer profile. There is generally a relationship that builds between the brand (seller) and the retailer/client (buyer). Savvy brands will research the sales and recommend range planning to the buyer to whom they have sold in the past to maximize the effectiveness of getting their brands to market; few retailers stock all the lines offered by a brand. This type of buying does not normally involve the buyer with the initial development of the product or branded/designer range.

Branded buying is typically used by both small independent fashion shops/boutiques and large department stores like Selfridges, although the retailer's profits tend to be lower on this product due to the high wholesale pricing and the cost of brand marketing. Private label buying, on the other hand, requires a much more creative and original approach than buying or selecting product from a branded range. Here, the buyer is involved in assisting designers to create and develop ideas, after which they then select the garments/products suitable for the season's range. Each garment or product is unique, having been initially designed by either an external or an in-house designer or design team. Once lines are selected, it will be the buyer's job to ensure that the best cost price is achieved, the right factory is sourced, and a workable delivery date is negotiated.

Figures 1.10–1.14 National and private labels. National brands can be seen in specialty or department stores, whereas many retailers have become household brands in their own right – such as GAP, Superdry, Old Navy, Zara, and JD Sports.

A retailer's profits tend to be higher on this type of product, as they source bulk deliveries directly from the factory to achieve economies of scale, thus giving the keenest cost price. In many cases, retailers will provide what is known as 'the brand is the label', whereby only one brand exists in the retail shop and that label is also used as the company name. This branding type is seen in retailers such as Gap, H&M, and Pink. Private label brands can turn higher profits, but also take time and money to develop each season.

What is a fashion buyer?

A fashion buyer is the individual or group of individuals (the buying team) whose primary role is to purchase merchandise for a retail organization. They work diligently in researching trends; sourcing materials and/or product; creating seasonal buying plans; and working with outside vendors and designers to produce a range that will be distributed through a number of retail channels.

Fashion buyers often have more influence over and impact on the overall financial success of a business than do fashion designers themselves. Although designers are the starting point of any fashion product, it is the buyer who will select the final range that they believe has the best opportunity to drive sales for the retail organization and, therefore, also fulfil the targeted customers' needs and wants.

Three key factors prescribe the scope of the buyer's job description: how the retailer's organization is structured, the size of the retail operation that they are buying for, and product assortment.

Throughout the year, buyers work with designers to continually develop, edit, and reject ideas, samples, and/or brands from those originally considered, whittling down items for potential inclusion in the final range(s). Whether buying for their own shop or for a large chain, the real acid test of a fashion buyer comes down to seeing whether the product selected makes it onto the retail space and sells out at full retail price.

In reality, a buyer rarely (if ever) achieves a 100 per cent success or strike rate. There is always an element of any range that does not sell well and will require a price reduction to help move it out of the shop. This in turn reduces the overall profit level of the business and must be monitored to avoid future mistakes.

Qualifications and expectations

Fashion buying is a competitive business with applicants coming from a wide variety of educational backgrounds, and many different skills and attributes are required to become a successful fashion buyer. Human resources professionals in the fashion trade are always trying to find the magic formula when recruiting for buying roles: simply having a passion for the fashion industry is not enough.

Internationally, the number of fashion-related design, manufacturing, buying, marketing, and management courses is increasing exponentially. Some have a stronger business focus, while others are more design-related, but none gives any applicant automatic entry into a buying job. Your letter of application, a strong CV, personal drive, and a convincing interview will often be as important as having a relevant degree. A buyer's role requires an individual to adhere to the following:

- Be efficient, flexible, and positive.
- Provide a high level of critical/forward thinking.
- Be systematic and confident with numerical data.
- Work both independently and in groups.
- Be able to analyse sales trends.
- Understand current trends and foresee future trends across different markets.

Figure 1.15 The buyer and the designer review trend boards and lookbooks following a visit to an international 'Ready to Wear' trade show.

- Be commercial with the ability to make consumer-focused decisions.
- Appreciate diversity in society and diverse cultures.
- Use sustainable approaches to fashion and the industry.

Buying teams and their working environment

Buying and product teams come in all shapes and sizes depending on the number of stock-keeping units (SKUs) in their range (Figure 1.15); working long hours against strict deadlines is quite normal in a highly profit-motivated business. The buying team typically comprises the following key personnel:

- buyer
- assistant buyer
- buying admin assistant
- merchandiser
- assistant merchandiser
- merchandising admin assistant.

Buying offices are great spaces to work and the general state of organization and the atmosphere of a buying office can often be a good indicator as to the overall mood and ethos of a retail business. Buying floors are typically open-plan, and each product group will have a store for samples. There will be space allocated for fitting sessions with body forms and mirrors. Well-appointed departments will have metal parallel rails or grids fitted to all the spare wall space available. Grids enable complex products and ranges to be hung and viewed together for consideration.

Figure 1.16 The buying team.
Buyer and assistant buyer discuss colour swatches in order to prepare new lines for the forthcoming season.

Working with other trading roles

The fashion buyer's diary is generally packed with a host of internal and external meetings. Most buying offices plan weekly, monthly, and seasonal meetings well in advance of the season that they are buying for, also considering planned foreign and domestic buying trips. This is when strong communication with those playing other roles in the organization becomes imperative for a successful (and profitable) seasonal buying plan.

A buyer's good reputation in the trade is important, as they act as an ambassador for the business. It is therefore crucial for the fashion buyer to display a consistent, efficient, and friendly manner in all their dealings, while at the same time remaining commercial, professional, and firm in all negotiations. The fashion business is more about the people than the product.

Garment technologists

An essential conduit between the buying team and production, the garment technologist is not only responsible for fit but also product fit for purpose. Buyers rarely have a technological background or training, so they tend to rely heavily on their technologist to give guidance and advice on a wide variety of product suitability, durability, and reliability issues. A good buyer–technologist relationship is therefore imperative.

All garments and fabrics require testing before release to the consumer, requiring buyers to continually scrutinize, check, and sign off a wide variety of test reports during the course of

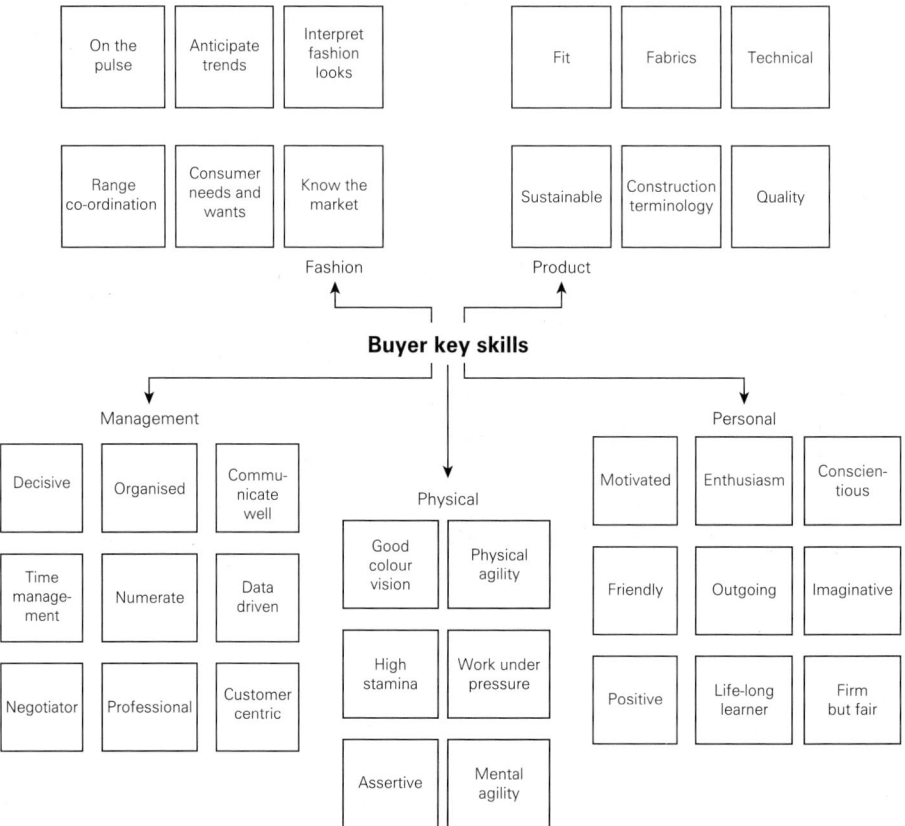

Figure 1.17 Key skills needed to become a fashion buyer.
The perfect buyer is an amalgamation of interpersonal and business skills and attributes, which change regularly depending upon the business context and the economic environment.

their work. Attention to detail is vital. Using internationally, nationally, and house-recognized product performance standards, buyers and their teams will work with their technologists to ensure that quality assurance standards are maintained (Figure 1.18). A buyer is also concerned with the health, safety, and welfare of the consumers who will purchase their products.

Planning and distribution

Although the planning and distribution departments tend to deal more with merchandising staff, from time to time fashion buyers inevitably become involved with both. Importing is a complex area and buyers who have good working relationships with both the planning and distribution

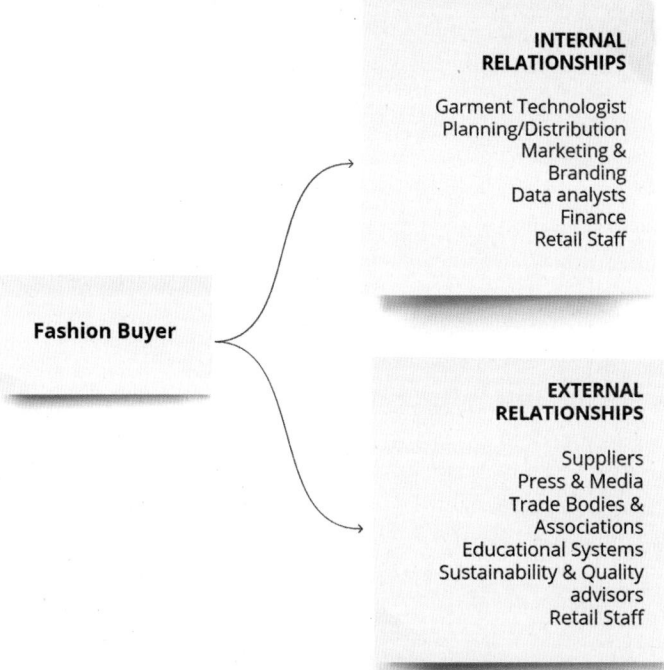

Figure 1.18 Being a team player.
A buyer must work with a wide range of colleagues and act as the go-to intermediary between those in corporate and supplier roles, streamlining and facilitating communication between them.

departments can often get their merchandise shipped faster and more efficiently. As buyers gain experience, the unique problems of importing unfold; if anything can go wrong it often does, even with a best-selling line!

Once imported merchandise arrives at the distribution centre (DC), it then needs to be moved to the retail outlets as fast as possible. Merchandisers are highly involved with the DC management and team, but again, experienced buyers often visit the DC to ensure that good relationships are maintained.

Fabric suppliers

Fabric accounts for the largest element of cost of a product – understanding fabric properties and influence is important for financial success. Although some buying offices have their own fabric buying team, in smaller businesses without a specialist, the buyer may meet with key fabric suppliers as well as garment suppliers. Having a thorough understanding of textile science is important for buyers regardless of whether they directly purchase their textiles or work with fabric suppliers, as they need to understand the performance wear and tear of their garments. Keeping abreast of new fabrics and technological advances is an extremely important buying attribute.

Marketing and branding

Larger fashion businesses have well-developed marketing and/or branding functions. Some businesses fully integrate the marketing and branding functions into the buying office; others keep them separate. Either way, the personnel involved will rely heavily upon the buying team to provide up-to-date information about new lines, hot sellers, problems, and other issues of direct concern.

Buyers may also provide help with photo shoots, press days, or other external marketing communications, though this is fairly uncommon. However, buyers help themselves, their ranges, and their trading performance by being helpful and available to assist with marketing and branding activities.

Press and media

Buyers are often asked to meet with their retail organization's press, publicity, or media personnel: getting a product into a magazine shoot can greatly increase sales. Buyers should be prepared to talk knowledgeably with their PR staff, which in turn will help them to write up a feature or review. Pre-season press shows are also held to showcase the new ranges to the media, at which buyers will be expected to attend to again talk knowledgeably about the range(s).

Trade bodies/associations and charities

A wide range of trade associations and organizations will approach buyers for help, information, and support. Some are legally based, such as trading standards and tax and customs; others are voluntary or socially based, such as trade-, national-, or locally- centred charities. The scope and scale of such requests vary by country. As any long-serving buyer will agree, everybody wants to meet the buyer, as they are seen as a pivotal and important point of contact.

Colleges and universities

Buyers are increasingly asked to deliver talks and to support a variety of academic institutions and fashion courses. Buyers will often work with universities to set live briefs and sponsored projects especially on subjects like diversity and inclusion, sustainability, and innovation. Working with universities also provides opportunities for internships and work experience supporting and developing the buyers of the future.

Fashion buying approaches and the consumer

There are several theories proposed for explaining why consumers purchase in the way that they do. However, most people agree that there are common underlying motives that prompt a consumer to purchase a specific item, which is typically reflected upon afterwards. Buyers need to understand these motives, along with other significant theories and approaches to consumer behaviour, in order to best capture their intended retail market.

The buying cycle – understanding consumer purchasing habits

One of the earliest (and most popular) theories of human motivation was proposed in the 1950s by Abraham Maslow, who discussed the idea of individuals moving through stages of growth, needing to fulfil each stage before moving to the next. Maslow identified the stages (in order of priority) as: physiological/psychological needs, safety and security, self-esteem, and love and belonging, leading to the desired goal of self-actualization (see Figure 1.19). Buyers can evaluate and gauge which stage their consumer market is in and create a seasonal buying plan and pricing strategy that correlates to it.

Another interesting model is the concept of decision-making theory (see Figure 1.20) which introduces a holistic approach that can be used to evaluate how consumers purchase goods. Though it is difficult to foresee individual buying choices, buyers can use this model to ensure that their purchases make it from the racks to the register more frequently, as well as for ensuring that issues such as quality, fit, and trend decline don't prevent the mass consumer from keeping the merchandise.

Being aware of approaches like the concept of decision-making theory will allow buyers to dig deeper into the mindset of their consumers, which can be used to better understand their own purchasing methodology. Then buyers can readily gauge whether they should make seasonal range purchases for a fast fashion market (discussed later in this chapter) or choose instead to invest in products of a more classic nature that will continually withstand the zeitgeist, depending on the department that they are purchasing for.

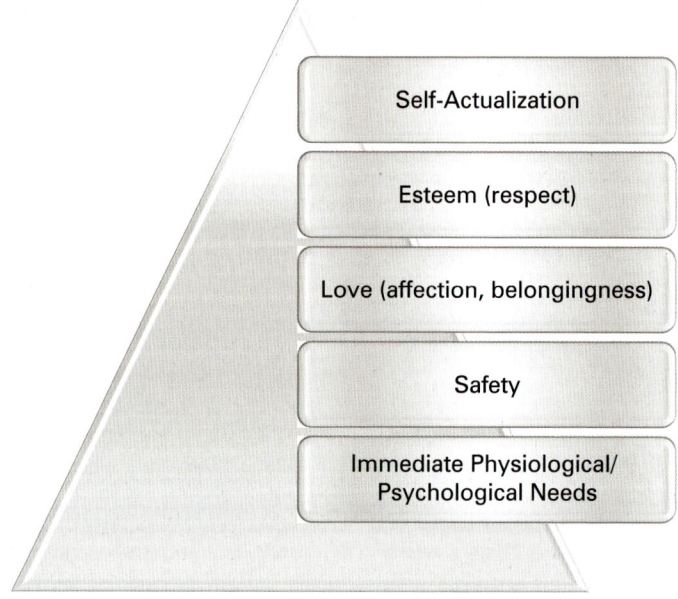

Figure 1.19 Maslow's Hierarchy of needs.

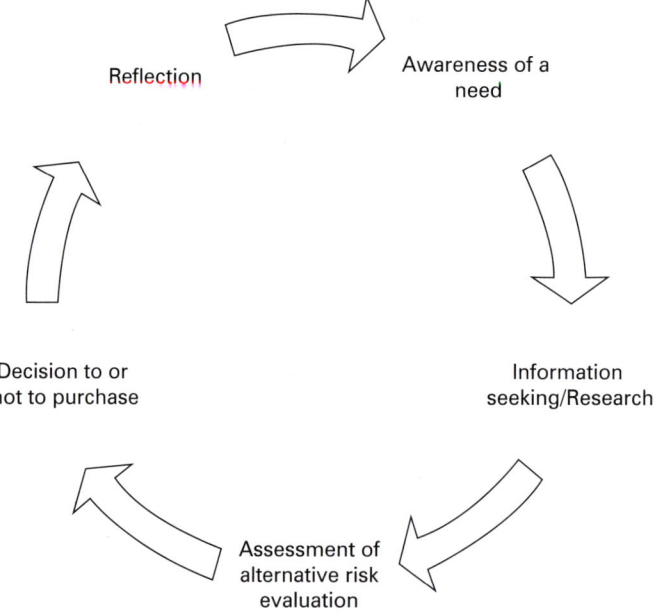

Figure 1.20 Simon's Decision making theory.

Fashion buyers use human behavioural theories to try to better understand their customers, such as Maslow's (1943) hierarchy of needs (Figure 1.19) and Simon's (1978) decision-making theory (Figure 1.20) which have long been studied for insight into the rationale behind consumer buying patterns.

Consumer Purchasing Motives

A strong buyer will be aware of the purchasing behaviours of their shoppers and will work to ensure that they are able to capture their market through a combination of the consumer purchasing motives detailed below:

Rational motives
These lie behind purchases that a consumer can justify as a need rather than a want. These items are rationally purchased and typically comprise everyday necessities. Consumers look at things such as quality, care, warranties, etc.

Emotional motives
Items are purchased based on an emotional response to an event in the consumer's life or by a feeling that a particular product gives them. For example, a woman purchases a new luxury handbag because she received a promotion and wants to fit the part. She doesn't really need the handbag, but excitement and a potential higher salary prompt her to purchase it. These purchases usually provide the feeling of prestige, status, or recognition.

Patronage motives
This is used to describe situations when consumers purchase goods based on personal preferences, such as brand loyalty or customer service. Consumers with patronage motives have a tendency to frequent the same retailers and become attached to them.

Understanding consumer markets

The global consumer has never been richer or more fashion-savvy than they are today. The exclusivity of fashionable clothing has diminished – society has democratized fashion so that it is now within easy reach of nearly everyone. People with style can find fashionable clothes at knockdown prices or resale sites, and fashion is not only achieved by buying expensive branded products. Intelligent fashion buyers therefore closely observe what people around them are wearing during their everyday business, social media exchanges, and social lives. Fashion trends often originate within society, whether in virtual or physical spaces such as shopping malls or bustling high streets. These diverse settings often serve as the starting point of fashion trends.

Understanding the modern consumer is becoming ever harder for the fashion buyer for numerous reasons, some of which are listed below:

- A wider range of fashion influences exist today, spread virally by social media.
- There is a media-hyped, ever-increasing faster demand for change and the new.
- People in developed economies generally have higher levels of disposable income.
- Increased levels of social connectivity between different cultural groups have led to greater levels of fashion awareness and a need to keep abreast of trends.
- Social and peer-group pressure is generated and stoked by popular media commentators, which encourages fast-changing trends.
- There has been a macro change from formal to casual dressing across the whole world – even in business environments.
- Fashion has become generally less gender-specific; androgynous dressing styles have been adopted more by both men and women.
- E-tailing and e-commerce has opened trade between overseas markets, making global trends more accessible.

Fashion buyers need to be fervent watchers of society and changing trends (Figures 1.21–1.25). Much of this type of personal research is informal, although frequently buyers, just like designers, will keep scrapbooks of photos, looks, and images to act as continuous sources of buying inspiration that they can later refer back to. It has even been known for buyers for one large fashion retailer to be paid to regularly attend nightclubs to ensure that they are up to date with what is being worn in street fashion and subcultures.

Figures 1.21–1.25 Style tribes.

Fashion styles today change at a more accelerated rate than ever before in history. Technology has enabled savvy fashion consumers to be both well informed and increasingly creative in their personal style choices and fashion purchases.

The fashion market, along with many other consumer markets, has fragmented as a result of larger social and cultural changes. In Western society today, consumers tend to form style tribes, preferring to create their own look or to be part of smaller trends rather than merely conforming to mass fashion movements. In the West, trends are generated by a society of individuals; in the East, society as a whole, and especially the family unit, is still highly valued, which has an impact on how fashion is consumed.

Fashion buyers therefore need to be continually aware of societal change and to watch trends and fads as they emerge at an increasingly faster rate. For today's fashion buyer, it has become imperative to understand the needs and wants of much smaller market segments, each of which ceaselessly changes and shifts in terms of brand allegiance and fashion taste. The day of one-look-for-all fashion is over.

> **Fashion changes, but style endures.**
>
> **Coco Chanel**

Fast fashion vs slow fashion

The term 'just in time' (or JIT) was used as a precursor to the term 'fast fashion', which is constantly used by the industry today. It emerged from a Japanese car manufacturing innovation, which shortened the lead time of supply chains, reduced inventory, and made supply very responsive to short-term demand.

There is no official definition of 'fast fashion'. It simply refers to trying to get the latest trend or other look out onto the shop floor at an affordable price and as fast as possible. 'Fast fashion' is a term used particularly when runway trends (especially couture) designs are reinterpreted by high-street or mainstream fashion businesses, usually at a fraction of the cost and in a matter of weeks. The idea behind this is that the shorter the lead time it takes to get a garment to the consumer, the less likely it is that competitors will already have a version of the same garment on sale. The fastest competitor to market should, in theory, reap a quick profit by being the first in, and hopefully out, of a new trend or product line. However, 'fast fashion' also poses a huge environmental problem as low-quality, mass-produced product rapidly ends up in landfill.

Getting in and out of a fashion look quickly is the sign of a good fashion buyer in this segment of the industry. This is because stocking the latest fashion look for too long, or as demand decreases, can leave a business with too much inventory that may then need to be sold with little or no profit. Most fashion companies therefore aim to continually use quick-response methods to meet consumer demands to shorten lead times and improve overall company efficiency.

The turnover of fashion is just so quick and so throwaway, and I think that is a big part of the problem. There is no longevity.

Alexander McQueen

Fast fashion has caused a destructive effect on the environment, retailers, and brands; encouraging consumers to buy cheap pieces that they wear once or twice then throw away may be good for profit, but the negative impact of over-consumption far outweighs the benefits of having the newest look. Slow fashion is the opposite mind-set and business strategy to the fast fashion phenomenon. Slow fashion brands typically use better quality materials that are natural, organic, and locally sourced. The design and making process and building in quality enables the product to have longevity and be worn season and season over. Slow fashion pieces are often re-sold, repaired, or have the ability to be recycled. Slow fashion is not cheap, the pieces are a wardrobe investment which adds value and appreciation to how the product is worn or used. Slow fashion brands include:

https://lucyandyak.com/

https://www.wearproclaim.com/

https://www.miakodanewyork.com/

https://theclassictshirt.com/

https://birdsong.london/

https://www.beaumontorganic.com/

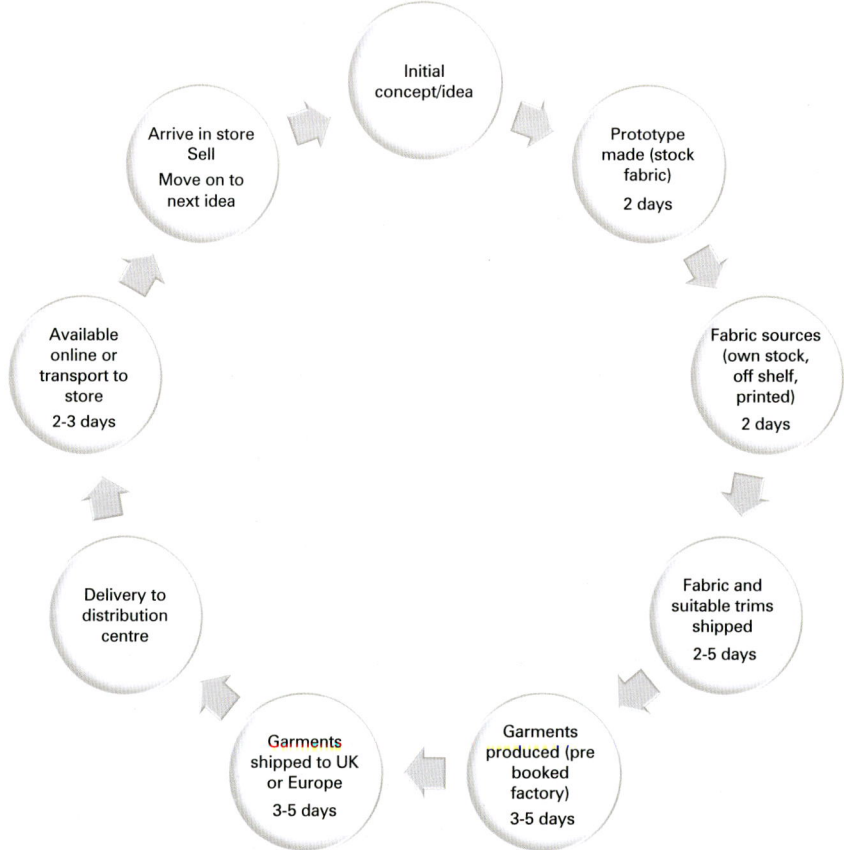

Figure 1.26 Fashion cycles.

Figure 1.26 is an example of the turnaround time for a fast fashion product. The quicker product gets to the trading floor the more likely it will meet the projected sales.

Product-specific purchasing

When buyers first enter the industry, most are placed in a department (womenswear, menswear, childrenswear, or home goods). They are then typically assigned a product class, such as knits, wovens, accessories, and so on to buy for each season.

Women's wardrobes generally contain many more garment types than do those of men or children. Internationally, women tend to spend two to three times more money annually on clothing than do men. There is no clear rationale for this, although the complexity of the female garment and product offer is often cited. In general, all clothing falls into two self-explanatory descriptors – formal or casual. Yet, societal change has created a demand for a far more casual approach to everyday dressing, with casual women's clothing now being accepted as the norm in many business settings.

Classification Hierarchy of Product Types

Different businesses, depending mainly on the size of their turnover, may put several product types under one buyer: for example, the jeans and trousers buyer. Similarly, many of the products in accessories are grouped together under one buyer. Every business uses its own classification hierarchy but, in general, the one detailed below for a dress is typical. Every line will also be given a unique line or SKU number for identification and IT purposes.

Gender	Womenswear
Type	Outerwear
Genre	Formal department dresses
Category	Eveningwear
Sub-category	Long evening dresses
Specific line	One style of evening wear
Size and colour	Specific size in specific colour/print

Basic Female Garment Types

Outerwear
Coats, jackets, ponchos, and suiting

Dresses
A-line, maxi, mini, and onesies

Tops
Blouses, button-downs, sleeveless, sweaters, T-shirts, and vests

Bottoms
Skirts, shorts, denim, trousers, culottes/capris, leggings, and jeggings

Accessories
Bags, belts, scarves, gloves, jewellery, hats, sunglasses, shoes, hosiery, and fashionable technology accessories

Intimates
Nightwear, underwear, and swimwear

Figure 1.27 Female style and garment types.

Figures 1.28–1.30 Female style and garment types.

Though buyers work independently on the specific class of garment that they are in charge of, they often communicate with one another to ensure that the purchases for the season can work interchangeably with all garment types.

Menswear

Menswear has far fewer different product types than does womenswear. Internationally, the formal tailored suit has given way to more casual dressing. Unlike women's fashion buying, men's fashions tend to be less extreme and there are less fast fashion brands and much more classic styles. However, the three main types of menswear are essentially similar to those of womenswear and consist of outerwear, accessories, and underwear.

Basic Male Garment Types

Outerwear
Suiting, coats, hoodies and jackets, trousers, jeans, shorts, and shirts

Tops
Button-downs, T-shirts, sweaters, sweatshirts, and vests

Bottoms
Denim, sports pants, trousers, and shorts

Accessories
Gloves, hats, scarves, belts, backpacks, ties, socks, jewellery, sunglasses, and fashionable technology accessories

Underwear
Loungewear, underwear, and swimwear

Figures 1.31–1.32 Menswear.

Figures 1.33–1.34 Menswear. Menswear today has become much less formal and more casual, with a clear move towards longevity, style, and femininity, creating the need for buyers to source and purchase more fashionable items, such as street style, athleisure, and gender neutrality.

Home goods/lifestyle accessories

Retailers are increasingly investing in lifestyle products for consumers, selling them alongside fashion apparel items (Figure 1.35). Buyers are quickly learning how these products parallel the fashion industry. Consumers today are rarely seen without their tablets or smartphones. With the traditional business office virtually obsolete these days, we are seeing a greater trend of lifestyle and/or tech accessories and small home goods in retail shops; from laptop cases to fashionable headphones.

Childrenswear

Childrenswear is probably the most complex, but least financially lucrative, buying area of all. Babies, toddlers, young children, preteens, and teenagers all have different wardrobes (Figures 1.36–1.38). Children's products are sold using various combinations of size, age, and height. However, this section of the marketplace is being highly influenced by social media and the online gaming society and will be excited to lead in to the areas of virtual fashion in the future.

Figure 1.35 Home goods/lifestyle accessories.

Many retailers today are incorporating home goods and small accessories in their shops, creating the idea of lifestyle shopping, as in this H&M store.

Figures 1.36–1.38 Children's fashion.

CASE STUDY
The Global Buying Director: Andrew Searson – Adidas

Andrew Searson (Figure 1.39) started his fashion career at Manchester Metropolitan University where he achieved BSc First-class Honours in Fashion Buying and Merchandising at the industry renowned Hollings Faculty, now known as the Manchester Fashion Institute.

Upon graduation Andrew decided to remain in Manchester, the heart of fashion in the north of the United Kingdom, famous for the industrial revolution and voted third best city in the world by *Time Out* magazine in 2021. Successfully achieving a graduate role with UK brand High and Mighty in 2013, Andrew started to forge his career in fashion merchandising, driving KPIs and increasing profitability through sales growth. Having gained a solid year's experience, Andrew started to look further afield for his next fashion business opportunity, applying and successfully achieving the position of retail merchandise manager at luxury brand Karl Lagerfeld in Amsterdam in 2014. Andrew led a high performing team responsible for delivering and driving e-commerce, retail, and outlet performance through optimal merchandise planning, developing product that realized the needs of

Figure 1.39 Andrew Searson.

the consumer, reducing terminal stock and enabling range growth. Taking a volunteering sabbatical in 2018 Andrew moved to Toronto, CA to work for the AIDS Committee of Toronto, and the Toronto Wildlife Centre. Alongside his volunteer work, Andrew took a short-term senior merchandising contract to reform the accessories division with one of North America's largest designers, producers, and retailers of footwear and accessories designer brands. In 2019 Andrew returned to the Netherlands and secured the role of senior buying manager at Adidas, leading the team responsible for planning and executing merchandise strategy within Adidas EMEA (Europe, Middle East, and Africa), forecasting, planning, and executing seasonal plans to fuel KPIs, and enabling growth in net sales, improved margins, and significant reduction in terminal stock. Currently Andrew is director of global buying at Adidas, responsible for overseeing global e-commerce buys in all regions for lifestyle product with a key aim of maximizing return on investment and identifying areas for further development. Andrew works alongside market buyers and global product development teams to ensure the balance the commercial brand needs.

Q: What is the difference between a buyer and a merchandiser in terms of their contribution to strategic success?

Within Adidas the core merchandising functions sit much closer to the product teams than buying. We're quite downstream. Therefore, in terms of strategic success, the merchandiser plays a vital part; they are shaping the range, briefing the collection, and therefore need to be on top of the trends far earlier than the buyers do. Buyers play their role in terms of in-season feedback, pushing for commercial articles that might have been dropped or missed, but the buyers' role is much more geared towards net sales success over strategy.

Q: As you have been both a buyer and a merchandiser, is it easy to make the move between the two career paths?

For me, yes but I've worked as a retail buyer (range selection) mainly, so the transition has been easier. In fact, I'd say it's an advantage having known the 'other side', it allows you to be one step ahead. There are different skill sets for sure, but a lot of the work overlaps.

Q: How different is it working in the luxury sector against the sports sector?

Aside from team culture, the main difference is where we sit within the product lifecycle.

Within luxury, we wanted early adopters – trend setters, and therefore needed to be ahead of the trends. Within sportswear (certainly my size of org), we need trend of course but later in the product lifecycle. We need product to perform commercially. Sportswear is usually more technology driven, with the lifestyle arm being more driven by fashion trend but with athleisure being such a powerful trend the two are now very much intertwined. Saying that, with sustainability such a key topic for our industry the collaborations we're seeing with sportswear and luxury I think will see some interesting changes to ways of working, for both sectors ... it's an exciting space to watch.

Q: How do you source trends that impact your buying decisions?
Within Adidas, it is largely 'brand' dictated. We're also driven by our basics; the trend is more the cherry on the cake keeping the brand relevant, but the reality is it's usually a much much smaller part of the buy so risk of backing (or not!) the right trend isn't vital to overall success. Our range is usually very wide too, so we can 'dabble' amongst the various trends.

We source trends from the usual contenders: WGSN, catwalks, EDITED. Social media plays a bigger and bigger part, especially when it comes to fast moving trends. Over the years though I have seen a switch from product driven to marketing driven ... like it or not buyers, you need to buy into the marketing styles!

Q: How do you connect with your retail arm (Online or Stores) and how do you receive consumer feedback?
For eCom, consumer feedback is gathered through net promoter score (NPS) scoring, ratings, and reviews and call centres. The buyers stay close to this and track any issues. Actually, we're currently quite disconnected from our retail arm within digital, but with a DTC (direct-to-consumer) focus going forward that'll change.

Q: Does feedback from retail/consumers impact the decisions you make?
The good thing is that it makes you pause and think about it, but sometimes we need to think scale. We're trying to get our shoes on thousands of pairs of feet. Is this feedback from one consumer, is it really an issue? A lot of people won't leave feedback. The real factors that tend to impact our main decisions are net sales, returns, and margin/markdown. Consumer feedback is usually used anecdotally to support our decisions and usually those KPIs indicate where there are problems.

Q: Do you use data tools and do they impact purchasing decisions?
Yes, and more and more we are relying on it. Pre-season forecasting tools, size curve forecasting tools. Largely they are developed in-house working alongside a data science team to develop and shape the tools we need. All developed to predict sales. There will always be a role for a buyer within fashion product, but it's changing and becoming much more data driven and much less gut instinct.

Q: What tools and systems could you not live without to do your role?
Regardless which size company, Microsoft Excel! You can't beat it.

Q: What is the most challenging aspect?
Within all my roles the brand versus commercial 'battle' has always been a challenge. Not wanting to flood the market so our consumer grows tired of certain products, but also wanting to smash net sales targets.

Q: What is most rewarding?
I've never met a buyer who doesn't get excited when they back something everyone thought would be a dog and it sells! That's the best feeling.

Q: What advice would you give to those starting a career in fashion buying now?
Work in retail. It's invaluable experience. Get experience. It's a real battle to get internships but seek out any opportunity you can. When it comes to recruitment I always think 'if we don't give people a chance they'll never get the experience!' but when the chips are down and we have candidates who've got the office skills and the retail experience, and we're under pressure to deliver targets there isn't always the luxury of time to train people.

Network. The world is small. Scarily small. I did a short stint working in Canada, we did a company trip to Columbus, Ohio and I sat down for dinner with some US counterparts. We were chatting and the lady I sat next to was best friends with the head of dresses for GIII. One year previous I was buying from GIII dresses from Amsterdam and chatting with her best friend! So, make friends, build relationships, talk with as many people from the industry who will listen.

Chapter 1 summary

This chapter has examined the fashion retail environment and the importance of the buyer within retail and the fashion retail landscape. The fashion buyer's role is explained, looking at the core attributes needed and their contribution to profit is aligned with understanding the consumer and the product. The fashion buyer's role within the team is clarified and the ways in which the work differs for branded goods and own-label buyers is explored. The chapter concluded with a discussion on product classifications introducing womenswear, menswear, home goods, and childrenswear, as well as specialty buying markets.

Questions and discussion points

Having looked at what makes a successful fashion buyer and how and where they work in today's competitive marketplace, here are a few questions for you to consider further.

1 Do you think that you already possess some of the key skills and attributes needed to be a successful buyer? If so, what are they?

2 Which of the skills and attributes do you feel you would like to learn more about, and why?

3 Do you think that buying womenswear is easier than buying menswear or childrenswear? If yes, why is that?

4 When considering the difference between buying branded goods from existing brand/designer ranges or working with suppliers and designers to create a unique own-label range, which type of buying would be more personally satisfying to you, and why?

5 Do you think that fashion can only be bought in high-end designer and high-market level shops? Explain your answer.

6 What types of stores do you personally like to shop in, and why?

Exercises

1 Rank the skills and attributes indicated in Chapter 1 in order of importance, as if you were responsible for recruiting a buyer for a fashion business catering for 16- to 22-year-old female customers. List the reasons for your choice(s).

2 Undertake a trip with friends to your favourite shopping area and see if you can find examples of the different types of the fashion/clothing shops described in Chapter 1. Write down as many names as you can under each shop type.

3 Repeat question 2 for shops of the opposite gender – do you find this a harder task? Why might this be?

4 Go into a large department store and talk to shop sales staff – ask them to tell you about brands that you may have never heard of. During your conversations with them, find out which of these lines are own-label, branded/designer, or concession. See if you can find at least two examples of each.

5 Together with friends, choose your favourite three fashion shops, and write a few short sentences explaining what makes them so appealing to you. Is it the shop, the stock, the staff, and/or other factors that please you most?

6 Try to locate and visit a vintage/pre-worn shop or charity/thrift shop and list the description of items (if any) that you would consider buying and wearing. If none, explain your reasons why not in a written statement.

7 Review your wardrobe, identify product that you have never worn, why did you purchase it, how long will you keep it? Can it be re-purposed/sold? Analyse how many tops do you have to bottoms? Which products are slow fashion and valued? What will be in the next recycling bag?

Sources of Buying Inspiration 2

Fashion trends have constantly evolved over the course of history. Society has always been inspired by and copied the styles of celebrities – wealthy aristocrats and royalty, influencers, and style icons are not a new concept. In the past the initial widespread means of fashion communication were fashion magazines like *American Vogue*, which featured illustrations initially and later incorporated photographs. Subsequently, from the 1930s to 1950s, cinema and TV became the platforms to exhibit the latest trends. French, Italian, and particularly American films had huge global influence. Today, the internet, social media, digital innovation, and the metaverse have taken over the global influence of fashion and are at the forefront of business-to-business and customer-to-customer communication. The technological revolution has complicated the work of fashion buyers, who now must work even faster to receive, synthesize, develop, and process fashion trends, before eventually converting them into the look of the moment as best-selling topical fashion.

Figures 2.1–2.2 Timberland GreenStride™ global launch event. GreenStride™ is an eco-innovation featured in the brand's signature boots. The global launch coincided with a worldwide campaign honouring everyday visionaries who push boundaries and drive positive change.

Buyers and market intelligence

A buyer will be faced with many challenges, but one of the greatest by far is the ability to create a range that satisfies both the domestic and international markets. International brands often invest in buying teams for both national and international trade, ensuring that the target market is accurately reached in those locations.

At first it can be tricky to learn the lexicon associated with different markets and the positions within those markets. In the United States, for example, a head or senior buyer may also act as the merchandising manager for a gender, class, department, or more. In addition, the term 'merchandiser' can often refer to the person who oversees the allocation and distribution of product assortments, but could also be a role responsible for visual merchandising strategies (the creation of artistic displays to enhance the promotion and sale of goods). Alternatively, the merchandiser for a branded company could be responsible for expediting the purchase order and managing the critical path from order confirmation to delivery to store.

The key factor is that the buyer and merchandiser are essentially working to ensure the successful sale of their product. However, it is worth bearing in mind that the terms and meanings vary and/or can be used interchangeably depending on the retail organization that you are working for and the country that you are stationed in.

A significant difference for buyers to consider is the volatile nature of fashion and the falling and rising of market values. If a buyer is providing seasonal ranges for both domestic and international markets, they should be aware of financial issues that may affect the price of their goods being sold, such as whether one currency is worth more than that of another. Buyers should be aware of the ways in which market economies can dictate the pricing strategies for goods sold overseas. If the price point is consistent and does not consider international market fluctuation, an organization's profit could turn out to be much lower than anticipated.

Other factors that may impede upon a buyer's ability to do their job successfully are elements such as lead times for samples or product or for any other information that needs to travel from one country to another. Knowing if international markets impose taxes or tariffs on goods brought either into or out of your country is also vital.

Close communication between departments within the business is crucial; teamwork will support the buyer to make the right decisions that are core to the success of the business. Finance will support currency decisions and monitor fluctuations and the imports team and freight vendors will have the most up-to-date tariff and lead time data that will support decisions made on the country of source and supplier selection. The planning department will source consumer and market data that will influence quantity, colours, garment size, and purchasing time frames.

It is important that buyers consider directional theories of fashion change to understand how markets are influenced across varying consumer segments locally and internationally, in particular, to discover who started it, where it is heading, and how long the fashion trend will last (Figure 2.3). A trend may be introduced at the higher end of the market but then later be translated and adopted at a more affordable price by the lower end of the market (or vice versa). It is precisely this availability of fashion in a wider range of retail stores and the cross-fertilization between market sectors that has directly resulted in the creation of a variety of fashion buying jobs across the sector.

In 1899, Thorstein Veblen and in 1904, Georg Simmel developed the theory of directional change that impacts the modern Trickle effect. Trickle-down theory reflects the traditional adoption of copying and adapting from ready-to-wear catwalks and designers. The trickle-up theory considers how individual tribe styles or street fashion can influence high fashion, ready-to-wear, or design. In some cases, a trickle-across effect may occur whereby all subcultures adopt a trend simultaneously and rapidly. This typically results from the convergence of mass media channels and is often equally distributed across the fashion sectors.

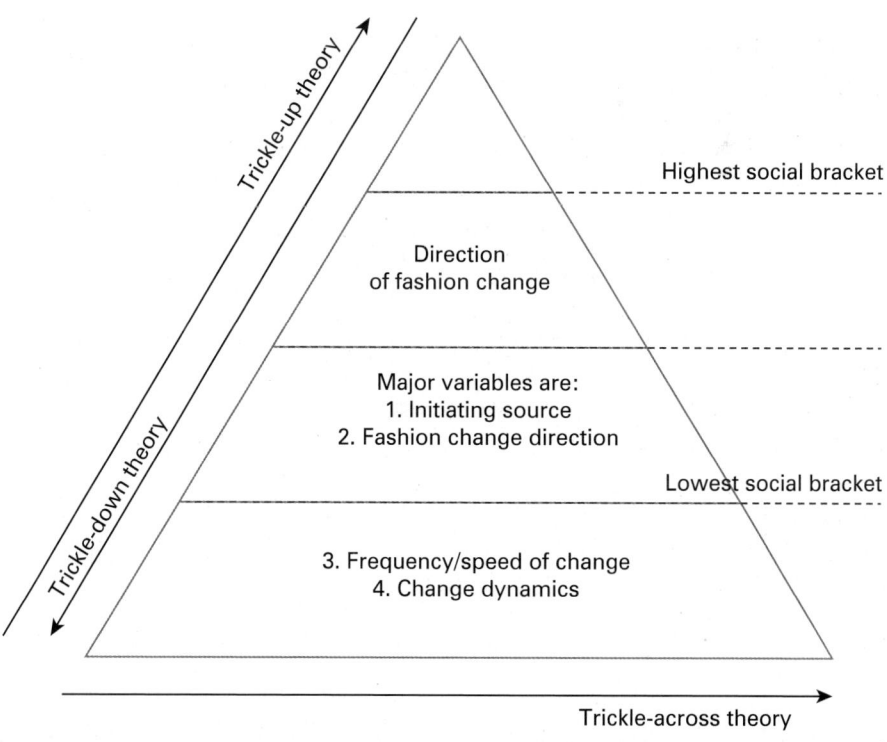

Figure 2.3 Directional fashion change theory.

The Fashion Buyer's Mantra

At all market levels, customers increasingly expect value for their money. Value is proportional to the relationship between quality and price. The key equation to remember is:

VALUE = QUALITY × PRICE

Figure 2.4 Fashion buyer's mantra.

Industry Insights

International trade associates and global news providers that provide a buyer with fashion industry insight.

Fashion Group International
An authority on all things business relating to fashion and retail design.

They provide individuals and companies with tools, thus enabling them to become more expert in their field.

VMSD
Retail design, merchandising, product knowledge, and industry news are their forte.

RDI

The Retail Design Institute promotes the advancement of and collaboration with retail environments.

NRF

The National Retail Federation has represented retail for over a century. Supporting retail to thrive, championing the people and policies that build success for retailers

International Foundation of Fashion Technology Institutes (IFFTI)

A global network of international fashion and textile institutes, who provide a meaningful voice, representing a diverse range of institutions from across the world (currently 61 institutions from 28 countries), offering an opportunity to share knowledge and intercultural understanding to inform, develop, shape, and direct the fashion and textile curricula and research agenda.

British Fashion Council (BFC)

British Fashion Council's mission is to strengthen British fashion in the global fashion economy as a leader in responsible creative businesses; empower and engage all within the British fashion industry to play their part in positive growth.

Fashion United

Fashion United is the industry's most trusted online global network for news, business intelligence, and jobs. Established in 1998, our independent platform is the go-to destination for a broad range of information and services connecting the global fashion community.

The Industry

The insights and intelligence destination for brands and retailers shaping the future of fashion https://www.theindustry.fashion/

Market research

Buyers are expected to undertake continuous market research using both informal and formal research techniques as well as qualitative and quantitative data. Informal sources of information are gathered through conversations with colleagues and stakeholders both within and outside the buyer's own organization.

Business meetings with external parties may provide buyers with inside information about their competitors and the trade in general. Often, such information can be used to the business's own advantage. However, it is important to remain an ethical business practitioner: be mindful that some insights provided about your competitors should remain with the external parties providing them.

The marketing mix

Marketing is a strategic process within the fashion industry; its core focus is to understand the consumer and create, communicate, and exchange a product that the consumer believes to have value. Customers in turn purchase the product and if there is value achieved they remain loyal to it through repeat purchases. It is important that the buyer understands their consumers and that range planning decisions are in line with consumer values. Good marketing is ultimately about creating long-term customer relationships. Professor Neil H. Borden of Harvard Business School drew upon this basic premise for what he called the 'marketing mix' in 1948. This basic marketing concept proposes that all good marketing is about placing the right product in the right place at the right price and then giving it the right promotion.

Although this might appear fairly simple, getting all aspects right in fashion marketing is not quite as easy as it sounds. Fashion buyers would generally not describe themselves as pure marketers, although they are in fact the main drivers of, and have the greatest influence on, the marketing mix of any fashion business. It is the fashion buyer who defines the product, has a major input into the retail pricing strategies, decides (in conjunction with the merchandiser) which outlets the products will be stocked in, and finally provides important input into any associated promotional activity.

For the buyer, the marketing mix is not a sufficient model on its own as shown in Figure 2.5 – buyers build a relationship between the marketing mix and buying five rights.

MARKET RESEARCH 43

Figure 2.5 Marketing mix and buying five rights.

Formal market research

The media shows a great interest in all things related to the fashion business, and fashion business stories are covered in the business sections of many international newspapers, such as the *Wall Street Journal* (USA) or *Financial Times* (UK). Buyers need to read these sources of media in order to be aware of financial and business matters concerning their competitors.

In addition to keeping abreast of the business and fashion news, many buyers may also have a dedicated marketing research manager who will help them to synthesize information with regular market updates, most likely using some of the regular marketing research reports that are available.

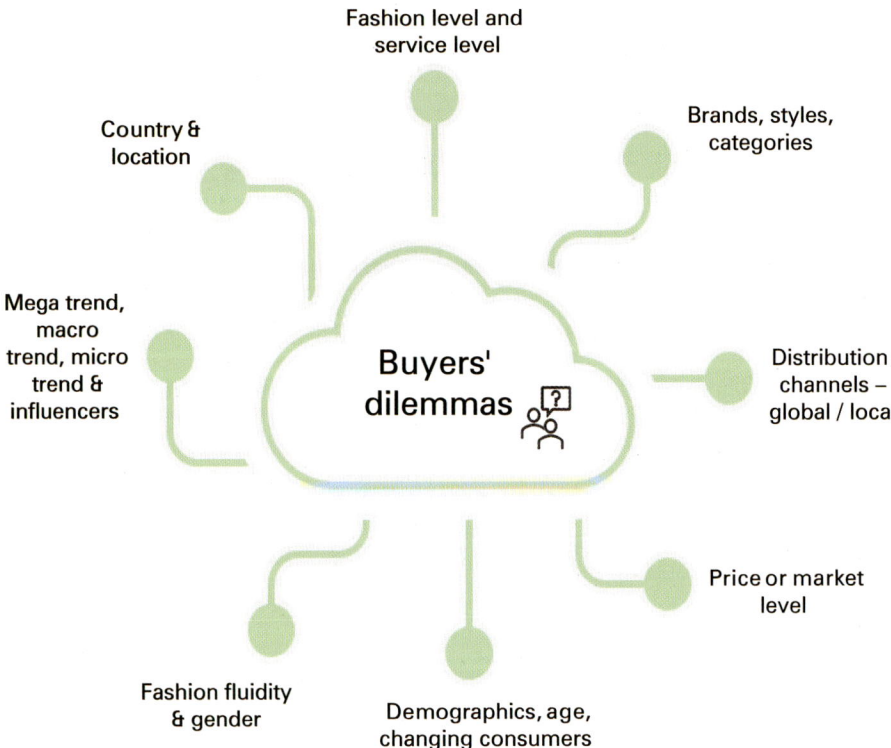

Figure 2.6 The buyer's dilemma.
Buyers are constantly faced with various market fragments and buying decisions that can weaken the brand image and cause marketing to become insignificant above. Using strong intuition combined with quantitative and qualitative data provided by both internal and external sources can help to strengthen a retailer's brand through the seasonal buys.

International Market Reports

Mintel
Providers of a wide range of international fashion reports; this is a paid service that is available in printed or electronic format. These reports are often available through academic libraries.

mintel.com/press-centre/press-releases/category/2/fashion

Verdict
Focusing on retail, Verdict provides a range of international fashion-related reports. Used mainly by companies.

http://www.verdictretail.com/

Euromonitor
Euromonitor is an internationally focused service that covers many business sectors, including fashion.

euromonitor.com

McKinsey & Company
In collaboration with The Business of Fashion, McKinsey & Company prepare annual forecasting and global market reports on 'The State of Fashion'.

https://www.mckinsey.com/

Focus on the customer

Good buying focuses on building a range that your customer will love; buyers need to ensure that they are making decisions that are in the consumer's interest and not their own taste. Successful buying decisions are underpinned by research, data, and information. This data comes from demographic and/or psychographic studies conducted either internally or externally.

The level of marketing research undertaken by different fashion companies varies enormously. Historically some businesses may have recruited small groups from their targeted audience (focus groups) to undertake semi-structured research into their opinions, attitudes, brand preferences, and buying habits. Fashion companies are now harvesting data through interactive websites and tracking devices that monitor consumer visits, shopping baskets, and browsing activities.

Other companies, depending upon the size of the organization, may take data that has been collected through loyalty cards and membership schemes.

Figures 2.7–2.9 Understanding your customer base.
Buyers look at their consumer segment, which provides demographic characteristics such as gender, age, ethnicity, and income, to put together a customer profile associated with a specific retailer.

This ensures that a business always understands its customers or potential customer base and supports their final decisions when planning a new range, providing a total picture of the new products that their targeted customers both want and need.

The omnipresence of smartphones and social networks is one of today's most powerful marketing tools. Social media is so much more than a tool for conversations with friends – it is an e-commerce tool. Social feeds and crowdsourcing for inspiration and acceptance are among the most powerful influences of buying habits in fashion and the ability to visually share product choices and looks has taken consumer inspiration to new heights, making or breaking a product range.

Consumer segmentation and quantitative market trends

Segmentation is an effective tool to align a product strategy with a consumer base. Demographic and psychographic data about spend per capita, broken down by gender, age, brand, and so on, is essential for the buyer to understand key socio-economic trends. Past, current, and projected sales performance is reviewed, often on a daily or weekly basis, to inform the buyer what is selling well and what is not. This data will inform buying or markdown decisions and impact the longevity of the product in the selling space.

Feedback from retail is also a source of consumer insight. Data will either reiterate what the home office and buying teams already know, or provide insights into changes occurring in their specific marketplace. Social media and interactive transactional websites allow buyers to respond to customer feedback at a rapid pace; consumer comments on online shopping platforms influence demographic consumer data. Consumers are asked to leave key information on age, gender, and location when they make a comment. Consumer-to-consumer communication crosses cultural boundaries and the environments surrounding them. This type of informal market research is essential in helping the buyer to understand how their customers dress.

Understanding a Retailer's Consumer Segmentation

Listed here is a range of marketing foundations that a buyer will typically use to further understand their consumer base.

Psychographics – a combination of both demographics and psychology that looks at consumer behaviour, values, and preferences.

Target audience – a segment of the consumer population identified by both demographics and psychographics, which enables a buyer to gain insights into the tangible and intangible attributes of a company's image, services, and/or products.

Differentiation – presents a company's image, services, and/or products in a way to best showcase their leading edge over others in their category.

Positioning – a marketing approach that uses target audience and differentiation to create a niche market for a retailer's brand, goods, or services.

> I design for real people. I think of our customers all the time. There is no virtue whatsoever in creating clothing or accessories that are not practical.
>
> Giorgio Armani

Customer profiling

Customer profiling is a marketing tool that allows retailers and brands to understand their customers, so they can offer a better product, experience, or service. Profiling is particularly important for targeting marketing activities, product development, and personalization, planning inventory, pricing, and the development and implementation of trends. Segmentation allows businesses to target specific customer groups; the data allows retailers to group common characteristics such as marital status, age, location; but profiling creates a perfect picture of the consumer who interacts with your product or service. Understanding the customer allows retailers and brands to target their campaigns and build brand loyalty. Retailers and brands look to convert consumers into long-term product ambassadors through a combination of social media and retailing initiatives, including sensory merchandising tactics, customer service, and, of course, new product and service offerings. Retailers and brands look for opportunities to widen their customer base outside the company's intended audience, capturing demographics that might otherwise be left to indirect competitors. To do this, they review valuable marketing data, which is obtained through both quantitative and qualitative research and environmental scanning. Identifying the current and potential customer base starts with basic demographic data.

Demographic–Ideal customer

You will hear quite often how retailers and brands use demographics to determine their customer market. Demographics look at socio-economic data such as age, income, marital status, and ethnicity (to name a few) and are statistical attributes gained by looking at the composition of a specific population. This information is used as quantitative data for scientific study or, in the retailer's case, marketing purposes. For instance, a children's retailer may look at how many households within a five-square mile radius of a proposed brick-and-mortar site have family members that are between the ages of 0 and 9 years. That same retailer may also look at how many of those households are married vs single parents. This information could be vital for the success of a store looking to venture out into new markets, specifically in the niche market of childrenswear.

Through the use of tools such as survey tools on social media, focus groups, website analytics, customer loyalty programmes, and POS data, retailers can learn valuable information that will allow them to create unique selling points specifically geared toward that consumer. This is how a retailer is able to provide a 'you may also like' up-selling area on their website, as it uses both explicit and implicit data collected to create a personalized e-tailing experience. Of course, it is imperative that retailers value quality or quantity so as to not overindulge the consumer with customizations that are not applicable.

Finding the right customer base to capture

Creating a solid customer acquisition strategy will allow retailers and brands to create memorable content that will resonate with each consumer based on their personal needs, as shown in Figure 2.10. Once a retailer acquires an audience, they must convert that new customer into a core/repeat customer through the utilization of customized content marketing and social media. Retailers also need to determine whether that core customer is of high value or low value; meaning, are they invested in the brand for the short term or long term?

Trend forecasting

Structured trend forecasting dates back to the 1970s, although fashion designers, manufacturers, and buyers prepared their own informal research long before then. Trend forecasting is an increasingly important function – getting fashion trends right can mean achieving the million-dollar line; however, getting it wrong is an expensive business – poor-selling stock requires prices to be reduced, thus reducing company profit.

Loyal customers: patronage-driven shoppers who prefer a specific brand or community that the brand cultivates.	**Discount customers:** price-driven shoppers who follow discounted prices, bargains, and/or sales.
Impulse customers: emotionally driven shoppers who buy based on their moods or feelings.	**Need-based customers:** need-driven shoppers whose purchases are based on necessity.

Customers

Figure 2.10 The four customer types.

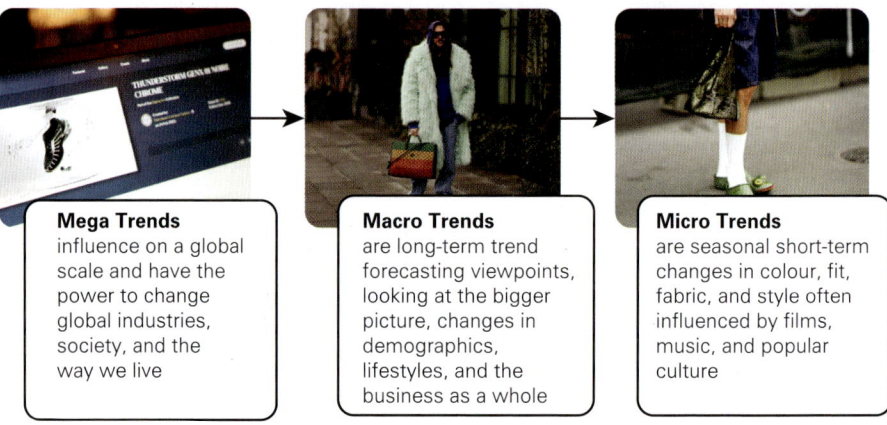

Mega Trends
influence on a global scale and have the power to change global industries, society, and the way we live

Macro Trends
are long-term trend forecasting viewpoints, looking at the bigger picture, changes in demographics, lifestyles, and the business as a whole

Micro Trends
are seasonal short-term changes in colour, fit, fabric, and style often influenced by films, music, and popular culture

Figure 2.11 Mega, macro, and micro trends.

Concepts, colour, and sources

The business of fashion is continually evolving, remaining in step with the up-to-date trends, and interpreting the trends in line with your customer profile permits efficient planning of production capacities and marketing campaigns that ultimately achieves significant market share. Figure 2.11 explains mega, macro, and micro trends, and the different scales that impact aspects of society, business, and culture.

The way in which each buyer assimilates trends has some commonality across different types of business. Larger companies often do this in a more ordered way, aligned with concepts and stories, smaller businesses are likely to take a more ad hoc approach, aligned with their core values and consumer choices. Larger companies are also more able to afford the services of relatively expensive external trend forecasting agencies, opting for the leading French trend forecasting agency, Peclers, or the increasingly influential UK-based Worth Global Style Network (WGSN). Most offer basic, expensive, and custom-made trend forecasting services and can provide forecasts for many seasons ahead, featuring concepts, stories, and themes of the future season. These are delivered either online or in a physical trend/lookbook format. The trend books carry clear colour illustrations, fabric swatches, or hanks of yarn, which are useful when discussing and developing ranges with a supplier. The development of digital technologies has diluted the complexities of trend research and there have been several pure online trend agencies utilizing artificial intelligence and offering cutting-edge trend research.

Trend agencies

Trendzoom

F-Trend

Eclectic Trends

Patternbank

Trend Council

Trendstop

Fashion Snoops

Like anyone working in fashion, a fashion buyer is subject to a variety of other trend influences, be these from an individual's personal life, meetings with colleagues, manufacturers, management, news events, or the wider fashion media. Throughout the year, buyers will also attend a variety of international fashion fairs, shows, and exhibitions, as well as local and overseas competition shopping research trips. Generally travelling with a designer, buyers will start to take notes and pictures to help them determine the direction of their future range, a process that leads to obtaining more formal marketing research.

Buying markets

The number of specialist trade events available for international fashion buyers to attend is expanding exponentially. Buyers working in larger fashion businesses will plan their attendance carefully, attending only those shows that are directly relevant to their product ranges in an effort to see the most innovative product. These are shows where product is wholesaled for buyers to either use in their production (i.e. fabric and trimmings) or finished garments to sell in their stores.

Trade exhibitions, fairs, and shows

Buyers, designers, merchandisers, and retailers will attend trade fairs and shows at specific times of the year that align with their seasonal planning and the global fashion calendar. Trade exhibitions are very large events, often involving hundreds of booths for vendors, manufacturers, suppliers;

Figure 2.12 Colour forecasting.

Many buyers will look at colour forecasting agencies such as Pantone, whose famous PMS (Pantone Matching System) is used for a wide variety of mediums from paper to fabric. Pantone's brand has become a leader in colour forecasting and is highly respected in the fashion industry, often collaborating with retailers – as seen with Uniqlo's cashmere collection.

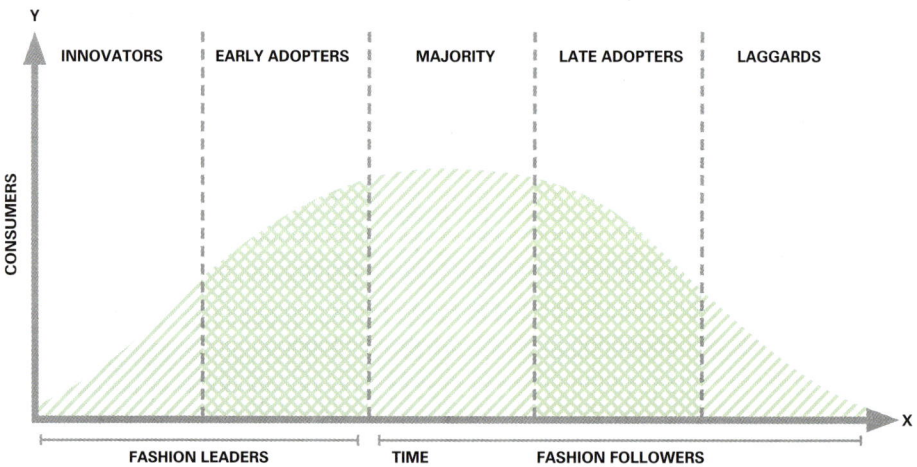

Figure 2.13 Diffusion of innovation.

Everette Rodgers introduced the idea of fashion diffusion in the 1960s. He stated that innovation needed to be presented to the public for approval and/or adoption. This graph explains the amount of time (X) it takes for this new innovation to be filtered through the population of consumers (Y) is the innovation life cycle. Buyers can use this theory to trend forecast the potential duration of a seasonal range.

therefore, it is important to plan your time effectively to ensure the visit is valuable and you achieve the business objectives of the trip. Trade exhibitions allow buyers to conduct essential market research, and source new products or routes to supply. Figure 2.15 details the essential research buyers gain from a trade fair visit. In a fast-changing market such as fashion, a trade show will allow buyers the crucial time to reflect on the current market situation and new technology, the impact of their brand, and become inspired by developments within the industry.

There will be stands, brands, or products that do not align with a buyer's product strategy, but will allow the opportunity for the buyer to encounter a new shade, texture, style, technology, or print that will provide inspiration for ideas for potential use in the future.

Buyers and designers may sketch garments or details that are new and innovative or take photographs as they navigate around an exhibition, keeping copious notes of show visits, along with relevant business cards and lookbooks from events. Note that sometimes using a camera is not permitted, so it may be worth checking with the show's organizers first, or the actual vendor.

No buyer can visit every stand, nor is it logical to visit existing suppliers who regularly visit head offices. It is essential to obtain a show or exhibition plan as soon as you arrive and to mark up and plan visits, mainly to new or potentially exciting stands.

Even with planning, the unexpected is likely to occur, such as when a new or exciting unseen brand or manufacturer is encountered for the first time.

With this in mind, a buyer must get as much information from the vendor as possible.

Line sheets are good to take away as they include detailed information on the product line being offered from the vendor, including contact information, delivery dates, garment flats, size range, colourways/fabric options, and, most importantly, wholesale and suggested retail pricing. Lookbooks also include aspiration imagery that showcases the seasonal concept; they also allow buyers to see possible styling options and give a greater sense of the target customer the line is intended for.

Buyers should be prepared to write and present a show report to their senior management team; this will include a review of the show, the shapes, silhouettes, colours, and textures of the season. They should identify successful brands/stands by commenting on which were busy and those that were unexpectedly quiet. It's essential to establish a feel for the market going forward and the brands/retailers to watch, as this supports decision making for your own brand/product range.

Why trade shows and fairs are so important for fashion buyers

Spending money and time at trade events must deliver direct benefit to the business, while enabling fashion buyers to:

- stay abreast of the latest developments and ranges of existing and new suppliers, brands, or designers;

- gather new ideas to help develop future ranges;
- network with other people, organizations, and businesses to ensure currency of own thinking and ideas;
- find new potential suppliers, brands, or designers not currently used;
- confirm that the ranges already developed and developing in the business are still relevant to the forthcoming season(s);
- potentially place orders – mainly for those buyers in smaller or independent businesses that buy designer and manufacturer brands.

Competition shopping

Many exhibitions and trade fairs are held in the fashion capitals of the world. It is normal for buyers to conduct competition research, fondly referred to as 'do the shops.' Comparative shopping trips can expose the buyer to new or previously undiscovered brands and shops, which can yield a plethora of ideas for future development. Buyers will purchase important or innovative products that they find to present ideas to their design and sales teams on their return to the buying office.

Figure 2.14 International trade shows and fairs.
Buyers will strategically visit a few key shows or fairs each season, identifying specialist and product-specific ranges that align with their product strategy. There are many vendors at these shows, and they compete to entice the buyer to choose their range for the next season.

The Trade Fair

Essential Research

Product Range and Quality: Getting a detailed comprehension of the brand's range. This will include the types of products they offer, the variety of styles, designs, and sizes available. Buyers will also review samples to assess the quality focusing on materials and construction and considering the overall craftsmanship.

Pricing and Terms: Knowing the pricing structure of the brand's products and any associated terms and conditions, such as minimum order quantities, payment terms, delivery lead times, and return policies. This information helps buyers evaluate the affordability and feasibility of working with the vendor.

Manufacturing Processes and Ethical Practices: It is important for buyers to ensure brands and retailers practise ethically and sustainably. Buyers will ask questions about the brand's sourcing and manufacturing processes labour practice, and environmental initiatives. Allowing the brand or retailer to show certifications or accreditations that demonstrate their commitment to responsible manufacturing.

Brand Alignment and Differentiation: Buyers can use the time on the stand to assess how the brand's products align with their own product identity and target market. Identify unique selling points, distinctive designs, innovative features. This can help to differentiate the product they offer in the market place and align the brand or products with their own overall retail, enhancing their competitive edge.

Market Trends and Insights: Trade fairs are a great opportunity to network to gain insights into market trends, emerging styles, and consumer preferences. Brands or suppliers who have a deep understanding of the fashion landscape, can provide trend forecasts, and offer valuable market intelligence.

References and Reputation: The trade fair will give the buyer a great opportunity to review the reputation of the brand or retailer by seeing them interact with other buyers. Buyers value vendors with a track record of reliability, professionalism, and customer satisfaction.

Production Capacity and Lead Times: Information on the brand's production capacity and lead times is essential, ensuring that they can meet the demand and timelines required for the upcoming and future seasons. Knowing the capabilities and capacity of a supplier will help the buyer to assess if they can manage order volumes and deliver on time.

Figure 2.15 Trade fairs vary widely in scope and format, to maximise the return on the investment from attending, a buyer must plan and set out achievable actions. Figure 2.15 outlines the critical research necessary for effective preparation and engagement during a trade fair visit.

Figure 2.16 Exhibition vendors.
Due to international competition, vendors spend a lot of time and money designing their booths to attract the next big retailer. Exhibition space is a big investment, as seen here; vendors will pay a hefty price tag for a booth that is close to entry/exit points and on corners or aisles.

Comparative shopping trips, like visiting trade fairs, need to be carefully structured. Often, trend forecasting agencies and the sales team at trade fairs will be able to provide buyers with a list of the contemporary retail outlets and shopping areas ahead of a foreign trip. Being out and about in a fashionable city also provides opportunities to spot new trends bubbling up at street level. This is also a great opportunity to begin the market research phase needed to introduce new brands to a retailer through the season's buying range. Competitive shopping will provide the buyer with the retail pricing structure of their competition and the product they offer. This is essential research for buyers as they initiate

Figure 2.17 Lookbooks and range plans.
Vendors provide crucial information for the retail buyers to ensure they have the essential information of their product offer, often using online applications and purchase order portals allowing buyers to place orders quickly and effortlessly and ensuring they get the lead time they require.

Figures 2.18–2.20 Understanding the global retail market.
In search of the next big line or key trend, buyers will often venture overseas and visit up-and-coming markets, identifying new brand opportunities or design inspiration, such as the Kanto Region in Japan or the Shanghai IFC Mall or the city markets of Ephesus, Turkey, and the fashion malls of Long Island.

their range plan comparative analysis, identifying product value, placement, and the intended consumer of a specific range.

Fashion weeks, trade fairs, and exhibitions are held biannually to enable designers and branded manufacturers of fibre, yarn, and fabric as well as garment manufacturers, to exhibit their next season's range to international buyers. They are generally held in January, February, and March, and again in September, October, and November to respectively showcase the following autumn/winter and spring/summer ranges.

Fibre, yarn, and fabric fairs

Fibre, yarn, and fabric fairs are the first in the exhibitions to occur in the fashion cycle, often taking place at least a year ahead of the garment season. These shows benefit the private label buyers who are more likely to attend than branded buyers.

The most significant yarn fair is Pitti Filati in Florence. The most influential textile and fabric fairs are Indigo and Première Vision in Paris, Moda in Milan, and Intertextile in Shanghai. Chinese and Indian fairs will no doubt significantly increase in importance over the next decade. Advances in digital material visualization are making it possible to see the authentic appearance of fabric texture and drape on a screen allowing the once tactile methods of fabric and yarn sourcing to blend into the digital era. Fashion technology and material scanning experts to look out for include:

Style 3D Fashion 3.0

Clo3D – CLO | 3D Fashion Design Software

Browzwear

XRite

Vizoo

Swatchbook

International fashion weeks

The main cities influencing international fashion are Paris for womenswear and Milan for menswear. The other important international fashion weeks are those held in New York, Tokyo, Berlin, and London, although debate rages each season as to which is the most influential. There are many more countries hosting fashion weeks – the list increases every year. Garment production zones that host fashion weeks allow the buyer to see the latest global trends and visit production plants at the same time; fashion weeks in Hong Kong, Vietnam, Seoul, and Bangalore are great examples of this. It is important for buyers to support up-and-coming design and innovation – graduate fashion week is often another important event in the fashion calendar.

Fashion weeks are made up largely of a combination of runway shows and static exhibitions, with events usually spread across cities in a variety of prestigious locations. They tend to attract the smaller independent and boutique buyer, as well as a varied coterie of other fashionistas, influencers, bloggers, and industry figures, including the international fashion press. Buyers from larger retail organizations buying branded own-label and designer lines are also in attendance.

International ready-to-wear trade fairs

These biannual events are generally held in large exhibition halls or on specialist trade exhibition sites. They typically consist of static stands with displays, with some fashion being shown on live models.

Generally running for four to five days, they attract a wide audience with both independent/small-store buyers attending alongside buyers from the larger groups.

Key fairs and cities include Prêt à Porter in Paris; CPD in Düsseldorf; PREMIUM Berlin; MAGIC in Las Vegas; FaW in Tokyo; Pitti Uomo, Pitti Bimbo, and Modaprima in Florence; and Pure in London.

Some shows specialize in one product, some are unisex or focus solely on childrenswear, while others aim to attract younger and edgier buyers. These shows attract brand manufacturers from all over the world, although some aim to attract more home producers.

Smaller businesses will actually place orders at these shows, while larger own-label buyers will undertake research, probably having placed production and orders much earlier with unbranded manufacturers. It is worth keeping in mind that a large proportion of the world's factories produce solely for own-label buyers and would not be represented at this type of fair.

1 North America

Mercedes-Benz Fashion Week
New York City, New York

Bridal Fashion Week
New York City, New York

Los Angeles Fashion Week
Los Angeles, California

World Mastercard Fashion Week
Toronto, Ontario

Mercedes-Benz Fashion Week
Mexico City, Mexico

2 Europe

Milano Menswear (Moda Uomo)
Milan, Italy

Ethical Fashion Show
Berlin, Germany

London Fashion Week
London, United Kingdom

Barcelona Bridal Week
Barcelona, Spain

Stockholm Fashion Week
Stockholm, Sweden

3 Asia

Hong Kong Fashion Week
Hong Kong, Hong Kong

Wills Lifestyle India Fashion Week
New Delhi, India

Mercedes-Benz Fashion Week
Tokyo, Japan

Seoul Fashion Week
Seoul, South Korea

Shanghai Fashion Week
Shanghai, China

4 South America

Senac-Rio Fashion Week
Rio de Janeiro, Brazil

Colombiatex de las Americas
Medellín, Colombia

Trinidad & Tobago Fashion Week
Port of Spain, Trinidad & Tobago

Fashion Rio
Rio de Janeiro, Brazil

Buenos Aires Fashion Week
Buenos Aires, Argentina

COMPETITION SHOPPING 61

5 Africa

South African DesynFestival
Cape Town, South Africa

Mercedes-Benz Fashion Week
Johannesburg, South Africa

Fashion Week Tunisia
Carthage, Tunisia

Dubai Fashion Week
Dubai, United Arab Emirates

The Hub of Africa Fashion Week
Addis Ababa, Ethiopia

6 South Pacific

Melbourne Fashion Week
Melbourne, Australia

iD Dunedin Fashion Week
Dunedin, New Zealand

Manila Fashion Week
Philippines

Rosemount Sydney Fashion Festival
Sydney, Australia

Figure 2.21 International fashion events.
There are many key events in the annual fashion calendar that take place all over the world. Buyers should familiarize themselves with these events and attend those that are most applicable for their work.

CASE STUDY

SEEK Berlin at Berlin Fashion Week: Damien Winpenny, Sales Manager, SEEK Tradeshow

Buyers attend trade events that showcase the latest designs and technological developments in apparel, accessories, cosmetics, and lifestyle goods. Trade fairs and events are seasonal and aligned with the product drop schedules of the fashion calendar. Buyers can browse a plethora of product and curate ranges, concepts and stories for their consumers. PREMIUM Group was an international biannual trading platform. Established in 2003, PREMIUM led the European show scene and is globally recognized for fashion, technology, and networking opportunities in a progressive and contemporary fashion industry. Shows included PREMIUM and SEEK, The Ground, and the future facing FASHIONTECH conference that hosts masterclasses on environmental issues, technology, innovation, and the future of fashion. At PREMIUM, buyers had the opportunity to engage with more than 1,000 brands and 1,800 collections, 30 per cent of the exhibitors will be new and upcoming labels, and 80 per cent international brands. Exhibiting 250+ brands, SEEK is a liberal and modern fashion tradeshow specializing in elevated sportswear, new classics, and true craftmanship, and upper street wear.

Figure 2.22 Berlin Fashion Week. PREMIUM Group Berlin and Damien Winpenny Sales Manager – SEEK Tradeshow.

FASHIONTECH is an interactive innovation space for fashion, technology, and lifestyle content. Using a completely new festival format, The Ground is where the best of fashion, lifestyle, culture, and diverse perspectives come together.

Founder Anita Tillmann established PREMIUM with a vision that would transform the uniform German fashion scene, introducing a platform that would showcase international fashion designer brands. Sadly, in November 2023, after twenty-one years, PREMIUM made the tough decision to close its doors and focus its energies on the SEEK trade show, evolving the show from menswear specialist brands to include contemporary womenswear and grow their Conscious Club. It is important for

Figure 2.23 The perfect combination of events and fashion.
Damien Winpenny, Senior Sales Manager – SEEK Tradeshow.

trade fairs to recognize that markets change and this is a fitting example of how to adjust your strategy and move forward into a new era in a positive way.

Damien started his fashion career in 2009. Whilst studying for his degree in Events Management, Damien worked as an assistant manager/buyer at the HIP store in Leeds, which provided the perfect platform to experience the contemporary cultural, street fashion scene and develop a foundation of retail-buying and sales experience live from the shop floor, whilst managing a portfolio of modern brands including Supreme, Engineered Garments, Adidas, Stüssy, Red Wing, Edwin, Woolrich, Yuketen, Maharishi, YMC, Oliver Spencer & more.

Graduating in 2012, Damien moved to London, taking a new role as buyer and retail manager for The Content Store. His focus, the development, acquisition, and execution of a portfolio of high-level brands from concept to live retail and e-commerce stores. Damien began attending international shows in a buying capacity including Pitti Uomo (Florence), Capsule (Paris), MAN (Paris), SEEK (Berlin), Jacket Required (London), and L:CM (London). In 2014 Damien became a wholesale manager for Brand Progression Ltd, developing modern menswear brands such as NEMEN, NEMEN x Acronym, Baracuta, Ebbets Field Flannels, Portuguese Flannel, Sandqvist (men's and women's), FDMTL, Hentsch Man, Far Afield, Fracap, Wild Bunch, Duffer Japan, Vanishing Elephant, Timothy Everest, Grunge John Orchestra Explosion, Uniformes Générale, and more.

In 2018 Damien moved to Berlin and joined PREMIUM GROUP as a sales manager at PREMIUM Exhibitions for the SEEK trade fair.

Q: What is your role at PREMIUM/SEEK? What does your daily routine entail?
I am responsible primarily for revenue and acquisition of brands. This includes developing the rela-

tionships with the current brand portfolio, maintaining and growth of existing business and reaching out to new and developing brands through market research, and social media. Focusing on account management I will use industry newsletters to introduce new brands to the marketplace, encouraging buyers to interact, network, and visit the show. Discovering and supporting new brands is a core part of the ethos at PREMIUM and SEEK. Brands can use the application tool to put themselves forward for consideration; however, networking and social media play a big part in discovering the most contemporary brands across Europe and the world. Instagram is an integral tool for sales outreach that provides a portal into a brands world, unique aesthetics, and the stories that they are telling. I will use this research to engage new brands with the SEEK trade event and to push new brands out to the retailers and clients. My networking and account management strategy will inspire buyers and brands to attend SEEK where foundations for buyer and retailer partnership are laid. As the bi-annual events draw closer my role will pivot to a client management approach, providing the buyers and traders with crucial visitor data and retailer or brand lists – data that provides a clear oversight of the visitor demographics and the potential partner opportunities that may flourish through social activities and networking events.

Q: How is SEEK different from other fashion market tradeshows? What makes it unique?

SEEK is a contemporary trade show for the fashion industry; the mix of brands is what makes SEEK unique. A buyer will be able to buy artisan Japanese denim products and at the same time review and research technical sports ranges. SEEK will endeavour to match the brands with their top 100 store list so their buyers can focus and find the brands that matter to them. SEEK is pushing the global fashion calendar by showcasing brands of both genders in one show, bringing womenswear to the market earlier and contradicting the traditional show schedule. Uniquely SEEK is mixing and blending brands under one roof to give buyers an eclectic and diverse mix to ensure newness in product offer. SEEK initiated the Conscious Club allowing brands to showcase sustainable initiatives through panel talks and marketing and adding value to the buyer. Providing an inclusive space, SEEK will offer stands as small as five square metres to the contemporary designer or brand establishing their place in the market; at the same time, SEEK pulls the big named brands who command prime position in the show with stands up to two hundred square metres.

Q: How do you determine which brands are a good fit for showing at SEEK? Is there a specific demographic you look to cater to?
Understanding the customer persona is essential, as is understanding the brand fit for the show from a design point of view. We try to establish who brands work with, their price point and consistency within the portfolio, how well established they are, the potential of the brand in the fashion landscape. SEEK must ensure that new clients resonate with their audience. SEEK has an eclectic mix of brands that nod to the Generation Z demographic, who are excited to experience new brands but also loyal to some of the heritage brands such as Blundstone and Redwings who are re-establishing their brand with a new and younger consumer.

Q: Do you see any trends and market shifts that will influence the way shows like SEEK will move forward to 2030?
A major move for the industry is blending the genders, bringing men's, women's, and gender fluid product together in one show. SEEK are pioneering this change in the industry. SEEK brands are challenging the traditions of seasonal influence and presenting seasonless ranges that will maintain margins and avoid discounting, evading the traditional retailer set up of mid-season sales and discounts. SEEK brands are striding forward on fashion industry challenges around waste, product longevity, and brand value. Each show will focus on contemporary and new product lines that complement the core staples that the brands are known for, capitalizing the focus on key pieces and product developments. SEEK is a show known for new, innovative exciting product.

Q: How do you keep SEEK relevant for retailers who predominately use the internet as a channel for seasonal buying? How do you entice them to attend the show?
After each show we will look to improve the experience to ensure that we bring together an interesting and strong brand list. Desirable brands make the buyer's life easier, they can visit one location with 300 brands at SEEK and 600 brands at PREMIUM. Buyers like to be tangible, touch and feel, be creative and have human interaction. Using brand talks and opportunities to learn through educational talks, SEEK is connecting brands and providing a platform to network and discuss the industry, and the value that they add is important to sustain the fashion industry.

Q: What are SEEK's five-year/ten-year goals as a community?
SEEK will continue to grow but maintain a focused offering and look to solidify the community through supporting buyers through workshops, panel talks, and developing a buyers' networking platform to share buying best practice.

Chapter 2 summary

This chapter has examined the sources of both formal and informal trend information that buyers draw on in order to develop their future ranges. The increasing use of trend forecasting services has occurred as a result of technology, which has enabled ideas and images to be globally transmitted in an instant. There is, of course, no magic formula to trend forecasting that ensures that all the lines selected will become best-selling lines. Ultimately, it all comes down to the skill and ingenuity of the buyer who is responsible for reviewing, synthesizing, and then interpreting the huge amounts of both formal and informal trend information available to them. Buyers should not simply look at things around them – they should see them as well!

Questions and discussion points

To be a good fashion buyer requires a high level of visual literacy and good colour vision acuity. Buyers need to be able to look at hundreds of fabric swatches, garments, and ranges and successfully synthesize information, such as style details, about them. Buyers then use this information to develop future ranges with designers and manufacturers. Successful buyers necessarily develop strong observational awareness and recall.

1. There are many similarities and differences within the international buying market. Based on your country of residence, think about the similarities and differences that exist between foreign markets and your own. Provide a list that clearly defines each and make notes on why these similarities or differences may occur.

2. Trend analysis is an integral part of the buyer's role and trends can be sectioned into specific areas: mega trends, macro trends, and micro trends. Looking back, identify an example of each of the three trend categories and what its impact on the fashion landscape has been.

Exercises

1 Working in teams or your friendship group, visit your favourite fashion store. Once you get there, identify a range, brand, or product that you personally like and know well. While there, spend no more than ten minutes looking at it. Then leave the store and write a page of notes about your visit in a notebook. See how much information you can instantly recall – do you remember, for instance, the sizes, processes, fabrics, brand names, colours, or styles of the key items in the range?

2 On your way into work, college, or university, see if you can remember any of the clothes that a fellow passenger or pedestrian was wearing in detail. See if you can recall colours, fabrics, shapes, and accessories; then think about why you remembered that particular person's clothes. Were they unique or different in some way, or were they in keeping with a particular trend prevalent among a certain age group or sector of society? Write a half-page report explaining what made you recall this person and their style.

3 Visit your local high street and write a brief one-page report entitled: 'This season's main fashion looks, fabrics, and colours are … '. Use a heading for each section and include sketches, swatches, or magazine cuttings to flesh out the information.

4 Using online research and interactive websites try to draw together a trend board, showing the three main trends of the season, along with the key colours. Share your interpretation of the look on Pinterest or Instagram and try talking about them to your friends and followers; this is good practice, as buyers always have to be able to explain looks using trendboards and moodboards.

Suppliers, Sourcing, and Communication

3

In this chapter, we will delve into the crucial relationship between buyers and suppliers, exploring how to manage suppliers and their performance within the context of a changing global supply structure. When selecting suppliers, buyers must consider various aspects, and this chapter will examine how a supplier can influence quality, pricing, and production lead times. Additionally, buyers should also evaluate a supplier's reputation, expertise, production capabilities, and dedication to sustainable practices.

This chapter will explore how the buyer works with a variety of people and teams within the fashion business landscape, often providing a pivotal communication role in terms of the business's relationship with both internal departments and external agencies. We will discuss the crucial buyer–designer and quality assurance (QA) team relationship, how they work hand-in-hand to create the right seasonal mix and provide an overview of category management to final-line selection.

Finally, we explore the field of textile science, and the significance of buyers being aware of its importance is emphasized.

Figure 3.1 SS23 Womenswear Show, Naomi Campbell walks the runway for Alexander McQueen.

The fashion designer–buyer–quality assurance (QA) relationship

The buyer and designer relationship is one of close collaboration; together they must ensure that their products and range selections are aligned with the intended consumer. The buyer is responsible for selecting the items that will be sold and will influence the pricing strategy and the retail environment whilst the designer aligns the most appropriate trends and creates the clothing and accessories that will be sold. Both have the same goal to enhance sales and produce a profitable range that will enhance the brand's reputation.

The buyer–designer relationship is greatly influenced by the trading environment and can vary from business to business. Normally, each product category will have a product designer and buyer and together they will develop ideas and samples in line with the strategic direction of the brand. Large and premium brands often place more emphasis on design, with a head of design and a design team that is part of the senior leadership team. Smaller fashion businesses and fast fashion retailers often maintain relevance and keep costs down by employing smaller design teams that are supplemented by freelance designers to manage specific ranges or season drops. This flexibility can reap rewards as the freelance designer is often involved in many disciplines and is at the forefront of creativity.

Ahead of the buying season the buying team, design team and marketing professionals, regardless of whether they are internal or external, will meet to discuss the new trends and future direction of the total business. During these early stages, preliminary brainstorming is used, alongside trend forecasts provided by commissioned out-of-house trend forecasting agencies. Inspiration comes from all parties involved but primarily from the buyer and designer who will work together to project the greatest profit achievable from forecasted trends.

The ability to efficiently develop products and deliver seasonal collections is contingent on the strong collaboration between the buyer, designer, QA team, and the supplier network. Range development begins with a review of the previous season's range to pinpoint the products that performed well, often referred to as 'winners and losers', and a discussion to identify the internal and external factors that may have impacted product success. The buyer will research the competition, consumer groups, and emerging trends. The designer will use trend forecasting agencies to evaluate fashion trends analysing colour, shape, texture, silhouette, and emerging technology. The QA team will reflect and report quality issues from production and returns data that may have impacted the saleability and longevity of the product. The buyer, designer, and QA team will come together to review and assess the performance of suppliers during the past season and use this information to give feedback and improve future partnerships.

Working together the designer, buyer, and QA department will begin idea generation on a working range plan with fabric swatches and branding ideas that are sketched up into two-dimensional drawings before the sampling process begins (Figures 3.2–3.3).

Figures 3.2–3.3 The designer, buyer, and QA department collaborate on a working range plan.

The designer is responsible for converting 2D drawings (Figure 3.4) and concepts into approval and fit prototypes that resemble the product to be sold. There are only a small number of fashion businesses that can resource and maintain in-house sample production units; designers often rely on their suppliers to develop and make prototypes and approval samples that are used to evaluate product aesthetic and garment fit. To transform a design concept into a physical 3D product the supplier will require a detailed garment specification. The designer and QA department will compile the specifications needed for in-house designed garments that will provide the essential information for the tech pack that is sent to manufacturers to use in the production of their goods (Figure 3.5). A tech pack is an important tool used in the development and communication between designers and their production teams. Figure 3.6 explains the significance of the tech pack.

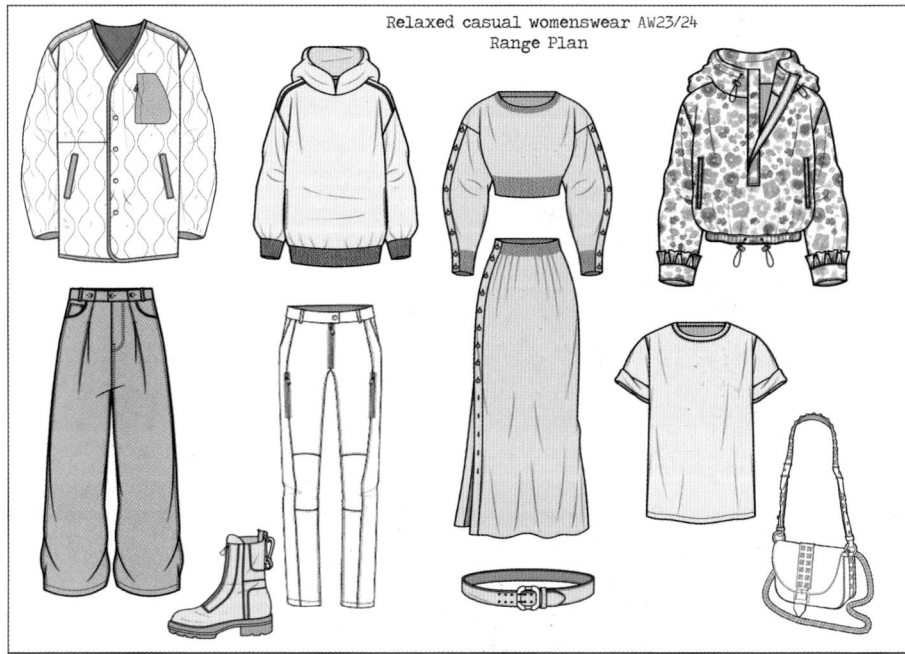

Figure 3.4 2D range plan.

There are many advanced technologies that are allowing designers to work with manufacturers on virtual sample processes, and in Chapter 5 this will be explained further through the case study on CLO Virtual Fashion Incorporated.

Designers spend a substantial proportion of their time researching and aligning their concepts and stories with the needs and wants of the consumer; they are influenced by trends in fashion, society, culture, and economic change. The designer will develop several products that will not make it past the first presentation stage of range planning, often a resource-intensive exercise. During the design phase, they must also factor in product circularity. Brands are increasingly integrating circular design principles across various product ranges and subcategories. A technology that will impact the role of both the designer and the garment tech is generative AI. This technology has the power to enhance the relationship between buyers, designers, technologists, and supply chain partners. Tools such as DALL-E, VisualHound, and Cala will become as mainstream as CLO and Adobe as businesses look to become resource efficient and tap into the plethora of images, design ideas, colours, and patterns available at the press of a button. In the future AI will have the capability to provide alternative inspiration to the extensive research and development needed in the preliminary stages of planning a range.

THE FASHION DESIGNER–BUYER–QUALITY ASSURANCE (QA) RELATIONSHIP

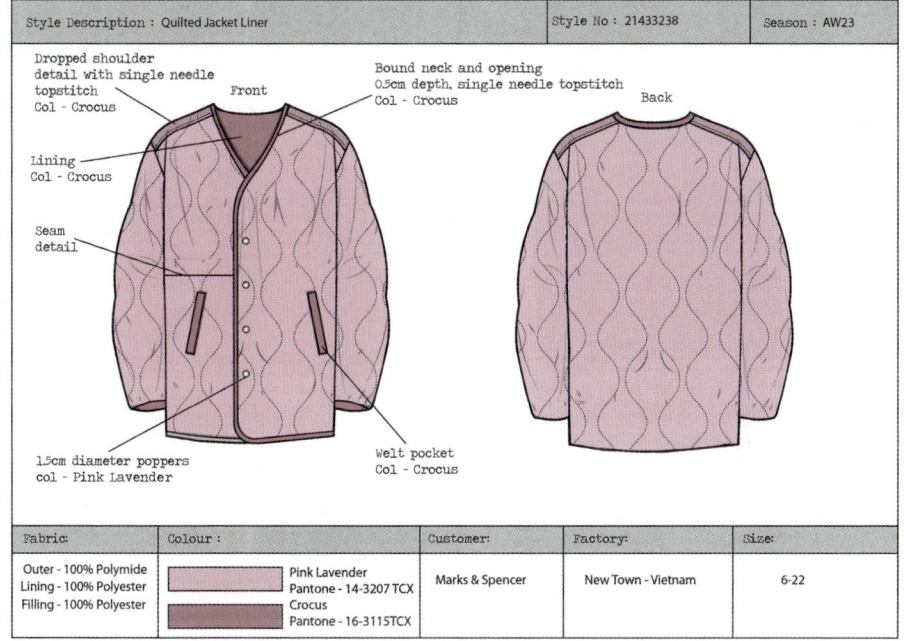

Figure 3.5 Extract from a garment specification or tech pack.

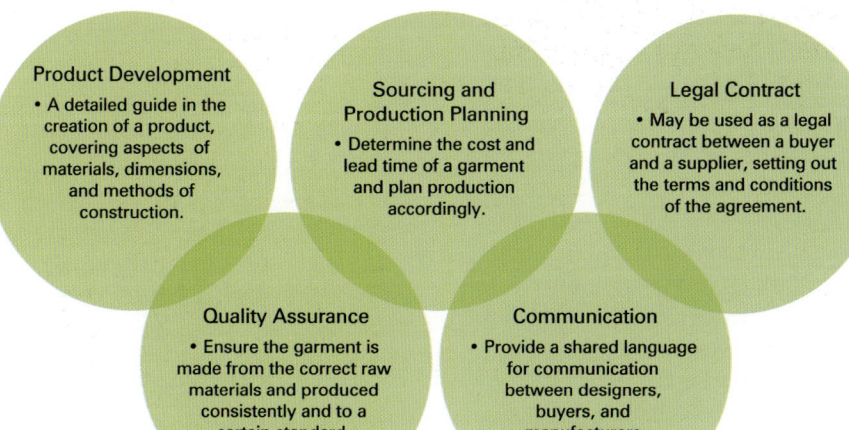

Figure 3.6 The significance of tech packs.

Information contained in a tech pack can include the following: (depending on the buyer and supplier relationships)

- Company/contact information/date
- Season/Drop number
- Designer/Product category
- Garment specification
- Graded block measurements
- Graded styling measurements
- Sample size and size range
- Colourways
- Main and trim fabrics
- Materials, trims, hardware, etc.
- Branding, labelling, and instructions
- Care labels, hang tags, etc.

A tech pack is crucial for ensuring that factories produce a brand or retailer's garment exactly as intended. The more detailed the tech pack is, the less room for error, especially when dealing with new suppliers or countries. In the preliminary range or product development stage, usually before the tech pack is completed, the buyer works with their supply chain partners, discussing possible product developments and manufacturing opportunities. This essential research will allow the buyer to gauge the impact on cost and raw material availability for new product creation, and determine whether the current suppliers have the skills and capability to support any product innovation. Buyers conduct extensive cost accounting or 'costing' to ensure they appropriately price their product. Costing looks at both direct and indirect costs associated with the manufacturing of the garment, enabling the buyer to determine the appropriate production, and selling prices.

What is a supply chain?

A fashion supply chain is made up of a sequence of activities that a fashion product goes through from its inception to its delivery to the customer (Figure 3.7). The supply chain usually starts with design and development and continues with the sourcing of raw materials and components, manufacturing, transportation, and logistics, as well as wholesale and retail distribution as shown in Figure 3.8. The buyer and supplier relationship involves the coordination and management of these activities. Fashion supply chains can include multiple partners, such as fabric and trim suppliers, garment manufacturers, finishing services, logistics providers, and retailers. The length and complexity of the supply chain varies dramatically according to market level and product construction. Lead times are influenced by product construction, fabric, and the location and capability of the manufacturing region, and can vary from three weeks to more than six months. Fashion supply chains require collaboration from various individuals, departments, and organizations not directly controlled by the fashion buyer. Usually, fashion retail companies do not own the entire retail supply chain, but instead have strategic partnerships with each member.

The buyer's role in the supply chain

The role of the buyer in the supply chain is vital as they serve as a liaison between the supplier and the business. They balance the needs of both parties to maintain a seamless operation. The buyer's key responsibility is range planning and

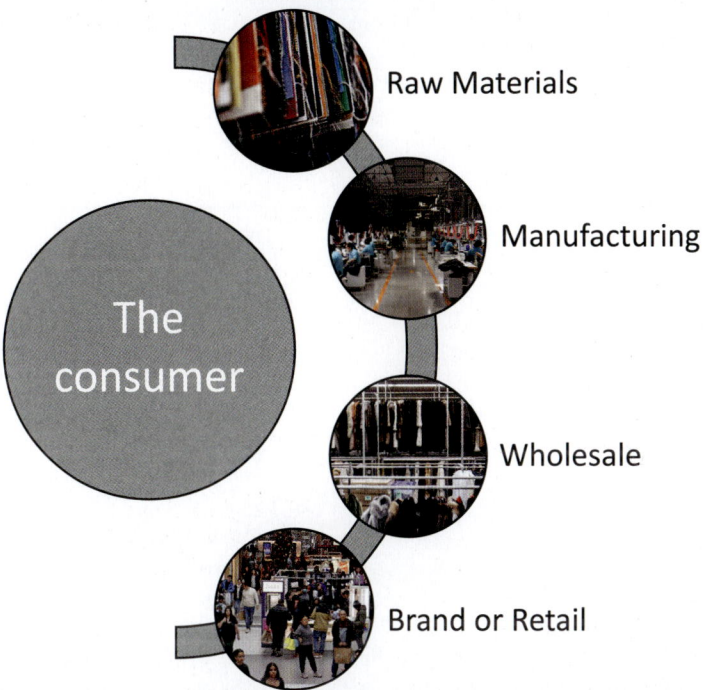

Figure 3.7 Shows the most simple activities of a supply chain.

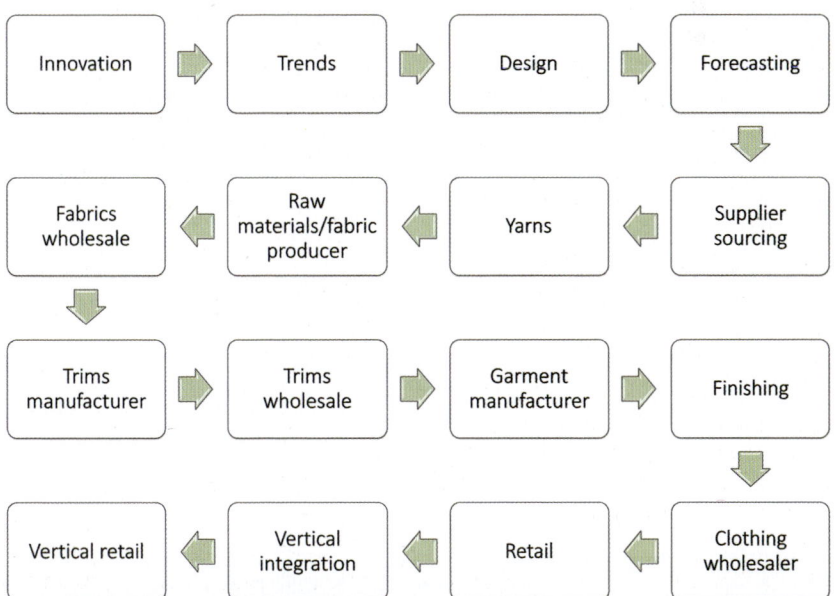

Figure 3.8 Supply channels to retail wholesale or brand.

Each supplier has a specific role (sometimes multiple roles) within the system, but each supplier's goal is to provide the consumer with goods and services, even if the consumer is the wholesaler or retailer.

confirming the final product selection for sale. They also make sure that the products meet the required cost and quality, and are scheduled to be delivered in line with the needs of the business. The buyer sources and manages suppliers, negotiates prices and terms, and monitors market trends and competitor activity that may impact the cost, the quality, and the availability of products.

The buyer's final decisions for the range and product selection impact the entire supply chain establishing critical path activities and the timelines. The buyer sets the direction and timelines for the core stakeholders. Decisions will determine the time frames for purchasing materials, fabrics, trims, and final garments; these decisions will impact production schedules in accordance with the selling period and the product launch, allowing the wider teams to plan product assortments, marketing strategies, and promotional incentives for the brand or store.

The Fashion Supply Chain

There are many retailers that act solely as the distributors of personal goods to the consumer, selling named brands that they have purchased through their wholesale network. The high street is also occupied by major brand retailers who design, develop, and produce their products through a network of suppliers. However, one notable exception to this rule is the Spanish company Inditex, owner of such famous brands as Zara, Zara Home, Pull & Bear, Massimo Dutti, Bershka, Stradivarius, Oysho, and Tempe. This company directly owns and controls a significant proportion of both its textile and garment supply chain and operates using a service integration model. Service integration provides a seamless integration of all the elements of the supply chain to enhance performance and customer satisfaction.

There are three types of service integration that can occur in this process:

1 Forward integration – to enhance customer experience and satisfaction by integrating product design, development, and marketing into the supply chain and providing both wholesale and retail operations.

2 Backward integration – to improve efficiency and cost by providing wholesale and/or manufacturing services that include logistics, and distribution.

3 Vertical integration – integrating the forward and backwards integration strategies from design idea to retail operation in order to meet the rapidly changing demands of the customers and to stay competitive in a fast-moving marketplace.

The buyer–supplier relationship

International fashion buyers have access to thousands of suppliers and brands, making the choice of the right supplier equally or even more crucial than selecting the bestselling product lines. A well-established supplier base and strong supplier relationships are essential for a successful fashion buyer.

Sourcing suppliers

The fashion industry is constantly under pressure to seek out ways to improve. Targets include cost, speed to market, quality, customer service, and sustainability. Fashion buyers therefore have a great deal to consider when working with suppliers, especially when introducing new ones. Traditionally, buyers would adopt a transactional approach, confirm range, select a vendor, negotiate a contract, and agree a cost (Figure 3.9).

To achieve business success buyers must approach supplier selection with a strategic mindset and consider the supplier as a partner that will help to achieve strategic change. The buyer will evaluate a supplier's technical proficiency, delivery times, quality, cost-effectiveness, customer support,

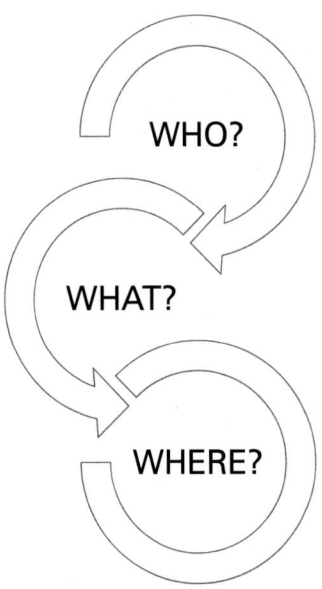

Figure 3.9 Who, What, Where? A transactional approach.

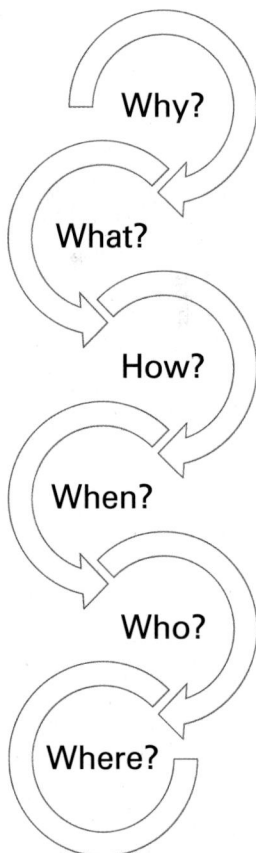

Figure 3.10 Questions for a strategic approach.

and their ability to produce product according to the brand standards. Pertinent to decision-making is the supplier's communication abilities both verbally and digitally, their sample production and handling capability, and their sustainable pattern drafting expertise. This view emphasizes clear objectives and transition planning and focuses on a more comprehensive decision sequence that is more likely to build long-term partnerships with reliable suppliers. Figure 3.10 exhibits a strategic approach.

Why? Supplier sourcing strategy: the range needs suppliers who operate at a specific cost, capability, or specialty.

What? Are we sourcing all products, some products, fabrics, trims, CMT, all services, functions of the business?

How? Completely outsource whole product operations or buy a finished product? Outsource the production, outsource the embroidery, or finishing?

When? In line with the season, the lead time, the product classification, local source, far shore, near shore?

Who? Who will be responsible and who makes decisions within the supply chain, buyer, merchandiser, imports manager, warehouse, operations director?

Where? Which country, which supplier, which factory, which agent, which wholesaler? How do you decide?

Buyers will look for suppliers who have invested in technology to support communication and product development. Technological advancements have dramatically transformed communication between the buyer and the supplier. Rapid exchange of data information and images has reduced the need to sample and has therefore reduced lead times. Remote conference calls have reduced the need to travel for meetings, enabling close collaboration on even the smallest product details. Buyers will also look for competitive advantage by selecting suppliers who have been awarded accreditations; the following list is a small example of what they can achieve.

SA8000 certified
Global Organic Textiles Standard (GOTS)
Fairtrade Certified Cotton
Better Cotton Initiative (BCI)
Organic Content Standard
Responsible Wool Standard
Oeko-Tex 100

How buyers and suppliers work together

Mutually setting expectations allows each party to work efficiently, in a successful partnership. Both buyers and suppliers must have open lines of communication, trust, and mutual respect, and an understanding of shared goals, expectations, and business processes.

An ideal supplier will deliver product to the highest quality within the negotiated price and time frame. To support the supplier to do this the buyer must clearly communicate design details, materials, and production schedules, and provide feedback on the final product. In return, the supplier will use their expertise in production and materials sourcing to suggest the best and most cost-effective methods of production.

Key Qualities to Look For in a Supplier's Representative

Like personal relationships, business relationships may experience challenges. In fashion buying it is desirable for a supplier to possess certain key qualities:

- Ability to take and act upon all instructions in an effective and efficient manner.
- Agility to support the buyer to achieve a faster time to market.
- Financial stability and potential to invest in product innovation.
- Technological compatibility to allow for hybrid working.
- Good, consistent, and accurate written, verbal, and electronic communication skills.
- Flexibility and the ability to support change.
- Creativity in interpretation relating to sample development in terms of line, range, and product category.
- A consistent and level temperament that remains cool under pressure.
- Confidentiality, the ability to keep commercially sensitive secrets from competitors and the trade in general.
- Good level of technical expertise and the ability to solve construction or quality issues.
- Honesty in all dealings, delivery dates, prices, issues, problems, everything to do with the business relationship.
- Understanding your brand and getting to know who your customer is.
- Overall personal efficiency, always following through on promises.
- A commitment to sustainability in products and processes.

Managing the supply base

Buyers are frequently approached by new suppliers seeking new business opportunities. These suppliers may be manufacturers, brand owners, or agents. However, buyers working for large companies will look for new suppliers when they have a valid need in their sourcing strategy. Buyers need to assess potential new suppliers; they often review more than they need in the search of a hidden gem. This informal supply chain research is a vital part of the buyer's role in meeting the needs of the business.

Buyers will use a variety of sources in the supplier selection process:

- Networking and word of mouth: relationships with other industry professionals, such as designers, agents, and manufacturers, can provide leads to new suppliers.

- Online resources: online platforms, such as fashion industry databases, websites, and forums, to research and find new suppliers. Good suppliers will ensure that their internet profile is clear and up to date.
- Direct approach by new suppliers aligning their product specialisms with yours.
- Referrals: recommendations from colleagues and existing suppliers can also lead to new sources of supply.
- Cold outreach: unsolicited pitches or cold calls from new suppliers seeking to establish a business relationship.
- Trade shows and events: attending fashion trade shows and events is a great way to meet potential new suppliers and see their products in person.

Monitoring supplier performance

A good buyer–supplier relationship can last for years but it can also last for just one season. Supplier performance monitoring is a crucial component of supply chain management, which involves continual evaluation of suppliers based on quality, delivery time, cost, and teamwork. To achieve effective supplier performance, it is necessary to establish clear performance metrics, use tools like scorecards and supplier surveys, and analyse performance data. Regular communication and a cooperative problem-solving approach are also important. The long-term goal is to establish a long-lasting, win–win relationship that contributes to the organization's success. Difficult choices must be made to maintain the integrity of the product's reputation.

Figure 3.11 Meeting the supplier.
To guarantee that the product meets the expectations of both the retailer and customers, choosing the right supplier is just as crucial as selecting the next top-selling fashion trend. Buyers browsing and meeting the suppliers at trade fair CurveNY.

Poor supplier performance can result in decreased business or the termination of the relationship. New suppliers to the business will typically undergo a formal approval process before being considered as an established supplier. However, for small trial purchases these requirements may be relaxed to promote efficiency and time. It is important to have a tight supplier network and buyers are under pressure to reduce the number of suppliers that they deal with in order to:

- Achieve economies of scale by buying more from fewer suppliers.
- Make business administration simpler.
- Improve the buyer's own time management.
- Make buying decision making less complicated.
- Develop buyer–supplier partnerships.

On-time delivery is key to success in fashion; a delayed order can miss a peak selling opportunity that can never be replaced. Advancements in technology has made it easier for suppliers to work SMART and suppliers will work with buyers or retailers to incorporate electronic data interchange (EDI) or radio-frequency identification (RFID) technology, which acts as a direct communication source between both parties. This allows for tasks such as automatic replenishment, ticketing, and return-to-vendor (RTVs).

Using both qualitative and quantitative performance criteria, buyers gain essential information on the performance of their suppliers and use this to make informed decisions about their supplier relationships. The combination of objective and subjective measures provides a balanced assessment of performance, essential for improving the performance of the supply chain and maintaining strong supplier relationships.

Quantitative performance criteria

- Delivery performance: the accuracy and timeliness of deliveries, including the number of on-time deliveries, the number of late deliveries, and the percentage of delivered items that meet quality standards.
- Quality performance: the quality of the products or services provided by the supplier. Including metrics such as the number of defects per unit, the number of returned products, and the percentage of items that meet the quality standards.
- Cost performance: the cost-effectiveness of the supplier's products or services, raw materials cost and handling, the cost per item, and the savings generated using the supplier's products or services.
- Responsiveness: the supplier's ability to respond quickly to the buyer's needs, including the time it takes to resolve production issues and/or complaints, and the time it takes to deliver products or services.
- Innovation: the supplier's ability to continuously improve and innovate its products or support services, including the number of new products or technologies introduced and the level of investment in research and development.

Qualitative performance criteria

Qualitative performance research will provide a complete picture of a supplier's performance by considering subjective factors such as communication, approach, and business practices.

- Communication: measures the supplier's ability to effectively communicate with the company, including responsiveness, accuracy, and the quality of information provided.
- Approach: measures the supplier's approach and willingness to work with the buyer or company, including flexibility, cooperation, and understanding of the end customer.
- Business practices: measures the supplier's ethical and responsible business practices, including environmental sustainability, labour practices, and management of the supply chain.
- Reliability: measures the supplier's ability to consistently deliver quality garments on time, including the operational stability and the reliability of its supply chain network.
- Flexibility: measures the supplier's ability to adapt to changes, including their ability to quickly respond to changes in the market and their ability to offer alternative solutions.

Sourcing issues

Fashion buyers need to keep up to date with global manufacturing shifts. Increasing complexity of the supply chain and growing pressure to comply with ethical and sustainable practices have led to the demand for specialist sourcing within head office operations (Figure 3.12). Advances in technology have made it easier for fashion buyers to access information on suppliers, products, and prices, allowing buyers to make better informed sourcing decisions. The growth of e-commerce and direct-to-consumer business models has increased the need for sourcing strategies that manage the logistics of moving products from suppliers to customers.

Manufacturing cheap clothing

There has been significant technological progress in the production of fashion products and the future will see the integration of robots and co-bots which will fundamentally transform the way that garments are made. However, the cost of implementing these advanced technologies can be high, and in certain countries the cost of labour is significantly lower than the cost of acquiring cutting-edge technology.

Fast fashion is the constant cycle of producing cheap and on-trend clothing at a rapid pace, where the priorities are speed and low cost over sustainability and quality. Fast fashion has negative impacts on the environment, directly contributing to excessive waste, pollution, and poor labour conditions. Economic history shows that countries with a cheap labour output eventually become more expensive, as workers become experienced and living standards rise. As shown in Figure 3.13, buyers face ethical dilemmas that should be further acknowledged and reviewed to ensure the health, safety, and welfare of all members of the supply chain, to meet a universal

Cost savings:
- Effective sourcing strategies will lead to significant cost savings. As a fashion buyer, you can pinpoint and communicate with vendors who provide top-quality merchandise at highly competitive rates.

Supply chain efficiency:
- Implementing strategic sourcing practices can enhance the efficiency of the supply chain. As a fashion buyer, you can collaborate with suppliers to simplify the production process, minimize lead times, and enhance delivery times.

Risk mitigation:
- Incorporating diversification into sourcing strategies can reduce the risks associated with relying on a single supplier. In the fashion industry, where trends and tastes can shift unexpectedly, this is particularly important.

Improved quality:
- Adopting a strategic sourcing approach can enhance the quality of products. Fashion buyers collaborate with suppliers to design and apply quality control measures, guaranteeing that goods conform to the necessary standards and are suitable for their intended use.

Improved supplier relationships:
- Employing a strategic sourcing approach can foster stronger bonds with suppliers. Through close collaboration, fashion buyers cultivate trust and establish enduring affiliations, which spurs greater teamwork and joint problem-solving.

Figure 3.12 Strategic sourcing strategies.

standard. Issues like child labour and slavery, pollution-caused manufacturing processes, and unequal/non-liveable wages are still factors that plague this industry. While buyers cannot educate the public on these issues, they can lower the risk of doing business with suppliers who engage in these activities through advanced supplier research.

Global sourcing

Global sourcing gives the buyer the opportunity to source the best combination of quality, price, delivery, and service from suppliers located anywhere in the world. Each area of the globe provides potential opportunities to produce quality, low-cost fashion goods, and buyers can mitigate risk by diversifying their supply chain and reducing dependence on single locations or supplier. There are several challenges to global sourcing, including cultural or language barriers, legal and regulatory issues, local laws, customs, and business practices, which all have the potential to cause buyers issues when sourcing globally.

> **Environmental impact:**
> - The fast fashion industry is known to be a major contributor to water and air pollution. Garment production often takes place in countries with lower environmental standards, leading to increased pollution and waste.

> **Labour conditions:**
> - Low-priced clothing is often produced in factories where workers are paid low wages and work long hours in poor working conditions. This leads to a lack of basic human rights for workers, including safe working conditions and fair pay.

> **Poor quality:**
> - Low quality materials keep costs low and manufacturers often use shortcuts in the production process, resulting in clothes that do not last.

> **Economic impact:**
> - Low-value production can also have a negative impact on the local economies. Businesses can reduce costs by outsourcing production in countries with low labour costs, but they may also be contributing to the decline of local industries.

> **Waste:**
> - Cheaper clothing is often only worn a few times and then discarded. This leads to increased landfill of textile waste. The fast fashion industry produces a significant amount of waste through the material choices and the materials used, and fast fashion clothing is often discarded after just a few wears.

Figure 3.13 The impact of manufacturing cheap clothing.

Asia

The following **Asian** countries are known for their advantageous combination of low labour costs, favourable government policies and large pools of skilled labour. As a result, many UK and US fashion brands have outsourced their production to lower-cost regions such as Asia, while maintaining their design and creative teams in local buying offices.

Bangladesh: known for its production of single jersey and cotton-based garments and is one of the world's largest exporters of clothing.

China: the largest production area of textiles and clothing in the world, known for efficiency in the supply chain and has vast production capabilities.

India: a rich history in textiles and apparel, a major producer of cotton and silk textiles, and a significant producer of synthetic and blended fabrics.

Vietnam: one of the fastest-growing garment producers in Asia with a flourishing reputation in footwear, lightweight, casual, and athletic wear.

Cambodia: another growing garment industry, particularly in the areas of knitwear and woven garments.

Indonesia: known for quality and a major producer of cotton and synthetic textiles, denim and outerwear.

Sri Lanka: known for technology and also a major producer of cotton and synthetic textiles in both knitwear and woven garments.

Western Europe

The origin of some of the most well-known luxury brands in the world with a long history of fashion; even though labour costs are high, the fashion industry is revitalizing as re-shoring and local sourcing is growing in the high-end product and classic styles.

Italy: known for luxury fashion production, particularly in areas such as leather goods, shoes, and accessories.

France: with Paris as the fashion capital of the world, it is known for design, particularly in the areas of haute couture and luxury fashion.

Germany: thriving fashion cities such as Berlin, Munich, and Hamburg are known for their production of technical textiles and functional clothing, as well as high-quality fashion production.

Spain: fast fashion capital and known to produce high-quality leather goods and shoes.

United Kingdom: known for heritage and luxury fashion design, particularly in the areas of tailoring, knitwear, and accessories. London is home to some of the world's most prestigious fashion schools, and UK-based brands such as Burberry and Alexander McQueen who are recognized globally. There is a manufacturing surge in the United Kingdom with high quality brands opening factories to develop the made in the UK label. Brands to look out for are Hiut Denim, Community Clothing, and Blackhorse Lane Atelier.

Eastern Europe

An increasingly important region for fashion production with a focus on quality and craftsmanship. Labour costs in Eastern Europe tend to be lower than in Western Europe, making it an attractive location for fashion production with the benefit of shorter lead times than Asia, providing a strategic advantage for brands looking to produce closer to key markets in Europe and the Middle East.

Romania and Poland: both have strong fashion industries with interests in knitwear, technical textiles, leather goods, and accessories.

Bulgaria: known for producing high-quality clothing and textiles, particularly in the areas of knitted and woven garments.

Hungary: a growing fashion industry, with a focus on high-end fashion production and design.

Ukraine: a large textile and clothing industry that pays particular attention to sustainability, with many brands utilizing eco-friendly materials and production techniques.

Turkey: with the fashion capital Istanbul, known for its high-quality production of textiles, leather goods, and ready-to-wear clothing. Turkish fashion brands such as Mavi, Koton, and LC Waikiki have become well-known in the global market and its location makes it attractive to both the Middle Eastern and European markets.

Africa and the Middle East

Africa is the continent with probably the greatest future and is an exciting prospect for fashion buying.

South Africa: the continent's largest manufacturing nation that is well established, producing high quality designs and garments and is home to several fashion weeks and events.

Nigeria: known for contemporary designs and local textile techniques.

Ethiopia: a long history of textile production that focuses on sustainable production and traditional craftsmanship, known for producing cotton and traditional woven fabrics.

Several North African countries (and former colonial outposts) are well-established sourcing hubs, notably Algeria, Morocco, and Tunisia. In the future, Africa is likely to become the largest garment- and textile-producing area with an abundance of low-cost labour; however, sourcing from Africa does present some challenges as many companies have limited infrastructures and poor access to capital for investment. **Middle Eastern** fashion is gaining recognition by engaging in fashion weeks, training programmes, and initiatives focused on promoting sustainable and ethical production. Known for its intricate details and luxurious fabric, buyers source from the UAE, Lebanon, Iran, and Israel.

The Americas

The fashion industry in the Americas is diverse and dynamic, with a range of established and emerging designers, brands, and garment manufacturers across North, Central, and South America. Like Europe, the Americas has seen a shift in production from the rich cotton producing areas to take advantage of the low labour costs and large pools of skilled labour. New York City remains a major fashion hub, home to a number of fashion schools and hosting many fashion weeks and events. **Mexico** has a strong tradition of textile production and is known for producing high-quality cotton and woven fabrics. **Brazil** has a growing fashion industry utilizing local materials and techniques. **Peru** is known for high quality Alpaca and other woollen fabrics, and **Canada** is pioneering contemporary and sustainable fashion with Toronto fashion week highlighted as one of the most important fashion events in the country.

However, there has been a push for onshoring in the United States, and, over the next few years, we will see this strengthen and begin to outbid other markets, if for nothing other than patronage motives.

SOURCING ISSUES 87

Figures 3.14–3.17 Global sourcing.

Fast fashion has shifted garment manufacturing towards the cheapest producing nations but consumers are pushing back due to the social and environmental downsides and near shore and local manufacturing are beginning to flourish.

Developing product categories and selecting lines

Due to the ever-evolving nature of fashion, buyers are required to plan well in advance of the selling season. In fact, they may be simultaneously working on several upcoming seasons, gathering inspiration for colour style and brand options, with another season drop in production and another retailing in store.

Lessons learnt

A crucial part of the seasonal phasing is identifying the lessons learnt from the previous range or phase. This review will identify what has sold well and the products with sales issues that needed to be marked down or phased out. Looking back to look forward, ensuring that each range will have the maximum selling capacity, the buyers will conduct a post-mortem report. The report aims to evaluate the performance of the buying plan and assess whether the targets set at the beginning of the season were met or not. Including a comprehensive review of sales data, stock levels, and margins, and an analysis of deliveries on time, the buying team will also analyse product categories to consider aspects such as colour, style, and brand performance, as well as orders and sizes produced.

The post-mortem report will also consider external factors such as market trends, consumer behaviour, and competitor activity to gain a broader understanding of the season's performance.

Choosing product categories

Product category management is the process where buyers will use sales and trend data to identify fashion product categories that are likely to experience growth or decline to pinpoint the 'on trend' or 'off trend' products of the up-and-coming season and ensure that the products that are included in the range align with the business product strategy and projections for turnover for the season and financial period. The first key part of the buying operation will be to decide which product categories should be developed and bought first, and in which seasonal drop they will appear. Consideration of lead times is important – those with longer lead times (for example, knitwear) need to be given priority over simpler, quick lead-time products such as single jersey or cut and sew cotton tops. However, nothing is guaranteed, and this part of the buying process is where the experienced buyer brings into play their ability to synthesize a multitude of information to produce the right category balance.

Selecting lines

The next stage in the process is to select the actual lines that make up each category. Following the research from the post-mortem report, the buyer will identify the winners and losers of the previous range and establish which lines to keep and the products that need to be replaced. Considering the product classification and category, there are often core staple products that remain unchanged apart from colour modifications to align with the evolving trends. There will be products that require a core product revision, possibly product to be re-positioned or removed and new product lines to add. The buyer will have a sales budget to meet and a buying budget to agree. This will be discussed further in Chapter 4.

The buyer must consider the retail environment and customer base to which the products are offered when determining the variety of products available, ensuring that both small and large retail operations have a range of options and balance. Deciding on the selection of products for small outlets or clients is particularly challenging, as there are limited options to meet the overall customer demand, and space for products is often restricted.

The buyer will work together with the wider team and use the sales budget targets to make edits and additions to the product lines, until a final range selection is made. During this process, it is crucial for the buyer and merchandiser to have discussions and reflect on their decisions, to establish a sales and buying forecast that will achieve the target budget. The next step involves matching the fibre, yarn, and fabrics with products that will be used in the final range selection, in order to achieve the desired overall look and silhouette for the upcoming season.

Selecting the Right Supplier to Develop Product Lines

The cost price of fabric, accessories, trims, and final garments is a key consideration for all types of fashion buying – negotiating the cheapest price is not always the most important objective. Fashion buyers also seek a range of other assurances when sourcing suppliers.

Product quality
Will the supplier (manufacturer or brand) deliver a product that meets the business's predefined quality standards – is it fit for purpose, will it wear, wash, and last? Poor quality can not only mean returns but also loss of reputation and brand value.

Shipments on time
Can the supplier make the product in time for it to be delivered for the planned selling period? Late deliveries result in loss of sales and more often the product needs to be marked down at the end of the season.

Product fashion level
Can the supplier efficiently interpret the fashion required? Does the brand offer the right level of fashionability? Contribution to product design and creativity is very important.

Communication efficiency
Does the supplier have the communication technology required to deliver SMART objectives and do they maintain regular communication with the buyer and their key support team?

Compatible technology
Does the supplier have the technological infrastructure to work with the buyer efficiently? 3D design

and virtual prototyping tools enable suppliers to create and visualize products in a digital environment, helping to speed up the design and sampling process; examples include Adobe Creative Cloud. Product lifecycle management (PLM) software allows suppliers to manage the entire product development process, from design and sourcing to production and distribution. Digital printing and textile design software enables suppliers to create custom prints and patterns digitally, reducing the need for traditional printing methods and minimizing waste; examples include Gerber or Lectra technologies and CLO.

Ethically managed production, carbon literacy, and sustainable values

Does the supplier manage their own sourcing and manufacturing ethically and sustainably? Do they consider their carbon footprint? Do they comply with labour laws and freedom of association rules? Do they have any sustainable accreditations?

Figure 3.18 100% Organic.
Fashion brands are switching to sustainable alternatives. French brand Jeans 1083, a 'made in France' brand manufacturing jeans in organic cotton.

Fabric selection

The fashion buying process begins by considering colour, fabric, and trends. In Chapter 2 we considered how trends and trend forecasting play a vital role in the decision-making process for buyers; after the style or 'look' of a range of garments has been established, fabric selection is typically one of the earliest decisions made in the buying calendar. This decision requires careful planning and thought, as the buyer must consider the garments to be created and select appropriate fabrics from the available range.

Fibre types

Fabrics are made up of either natural fibres that come from animals or plants (such as wool or cotton) or man-made fibres, which are typically made from mineral or synthetic-based chemical substances (such as acrylic or polyester). Often, several types of synthetic and natural fibres are blended together to create fabrics with a better appearance, hand, or functional properties.

Fabric types

There are two main types of fabric construction that are developed from knitting or weaving yarns, which are discussed in more detail below.

Knitted, woven, and bonded fabrics

Knitted fabrics are usually created by looping a single yarn or multiple yarns together. These looped yarns create horizontal and vertical connections, respectively called course and wale stitches. Woven fabrics are created when two yarns are interwoven together, with the warp yarn running down the length of a fabric and the weft yarn running across it. Bonded fabrics are often used for linings, while garment interlinings are created by simply sticking fibres together. Fabrics can be dyed either at the yarn stage or even at the finished fabric or garment stage, a technique known as 'piece dyeing'. Sometimes fabrics are held undyed in a 'greige' state, which allows buyers to make colour dyeing decisions closer to the season. It's unrealistic for a fashion buyer to have knowledge about every single fibre or yarn available in the market. However, most buyers possess a proficient understanding of textile science because they have to make critical decisions regarding the suitability of the fabric and yarn for the garments they buy.

Figure 3.19 Hand versus machine. Fabrics, and how they handle during manufacturing, vary a great deal. Technology is advancing in robots and co-bots, but so far the human hand of the machinist has not been replaced by either robots or machines.

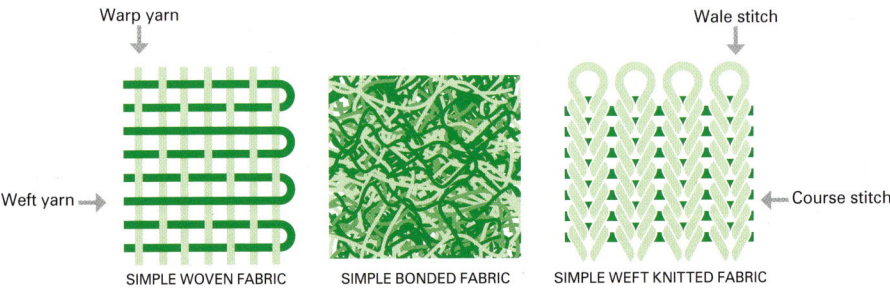

Figure 3.20 The three basic types of fabric.
Buyers need to remain constantly aware of new yarn and fabric developments, which improve the material that they have to work with. Technological advances in textiles have created some innovative (and expensive) options for the fashion market.

Printed fabrics

Prints come in every conceivable size, colour, and genre, so it is hardly surprising that print trends are frequently one of the key determining factors when planning a fashion range. The size, construction, and repeat length of a print can have a dramatic impact on the cost of a garment. This is particularly true with large prints, as during the matching/cutting processes, large areas of printed fabric may be wasted. Given the speed with which fashion trends travel, buyers often seek print exclusivity in order to give their range a competitive edge.

Fashion lead times and the fashion buying cycle

In line with the global fashion calendar, fabric manufacturers develop new fabrics, designs, prints, and looks at least twelve months prior to the season in which they will be made into a range of garments. Therefore, unless a fashion buyer is working for an extremely large organization, it is normal for

them to buy fabrics that have been already created for pre-existing ranges. Occasionally, however, some large-scale buyers will involve themselves with the design of a fabric from scratch. Specific colour and print decisions can normally be left to around six months ahead of the planned buying season.

Sourcing trips

Traditionally, fashion buyers would go on sourcing trips to both existing and potential new suppliers in key manufacturing areas twice a year. The development of technology and digital communication has allowed buyers to source products online or through virtual showrooms, reducing the need for physical travel. However, due to the tactile nature of fashion products, buyers often prefer to visit in-person sourcing events to see and feel the products, allowing the buyer to view and source new collections of yarns, fibres, fabrics, designs, and accessories for the upcoming season. The trips often coincide with global fashion and fabric events such as the Canton Fair in China, Premier Vision in Paris, Pitti

FASHION BUYERS AND FABRIC SOURCING

Figure 3.21 Sourcing fabrics.
Many manufacturers will have predesigned and manufactured textiles available for buyers to select from, making lead times much faster.

Immagine Uomo in Florence, or Magic in Las Vegas. Sourcing trips serve several purposes: the development of samples, planning, and outlining production and delivery, as well as the seeking out of new products, suppliers, and/or brands. At the same time, buyers will also try to visit interesting shopping areas in a foreign city to check out the competition and discover new and exciting products to bring into the fashion mix.

Foreign travel is seen by many as a perk of the job, although in reality it is very demanding, given the level of preplanning required and the intensity of the workload involved. Often, suppliers from outlying factories will agree to meet buyers in centrally based buying offices in order to help them maximize their working time. On occasion, merchandisers will join these trips, mainly for the purpose of production planning.

Fashion buyers and fabric sourcing

Fabric selection is crucial in the garment design process and can significantly impact the success of a product line. Opting for an innovative or durable fabric can give the product a competitive advantage and enhance its longevity. Moreover, sourcing innovative and sustainable fabrics can contribute to improving the overall sustainability of the product range. Fashion buyers continually research and explore new and innovative fabrics, often due to the increasing influence

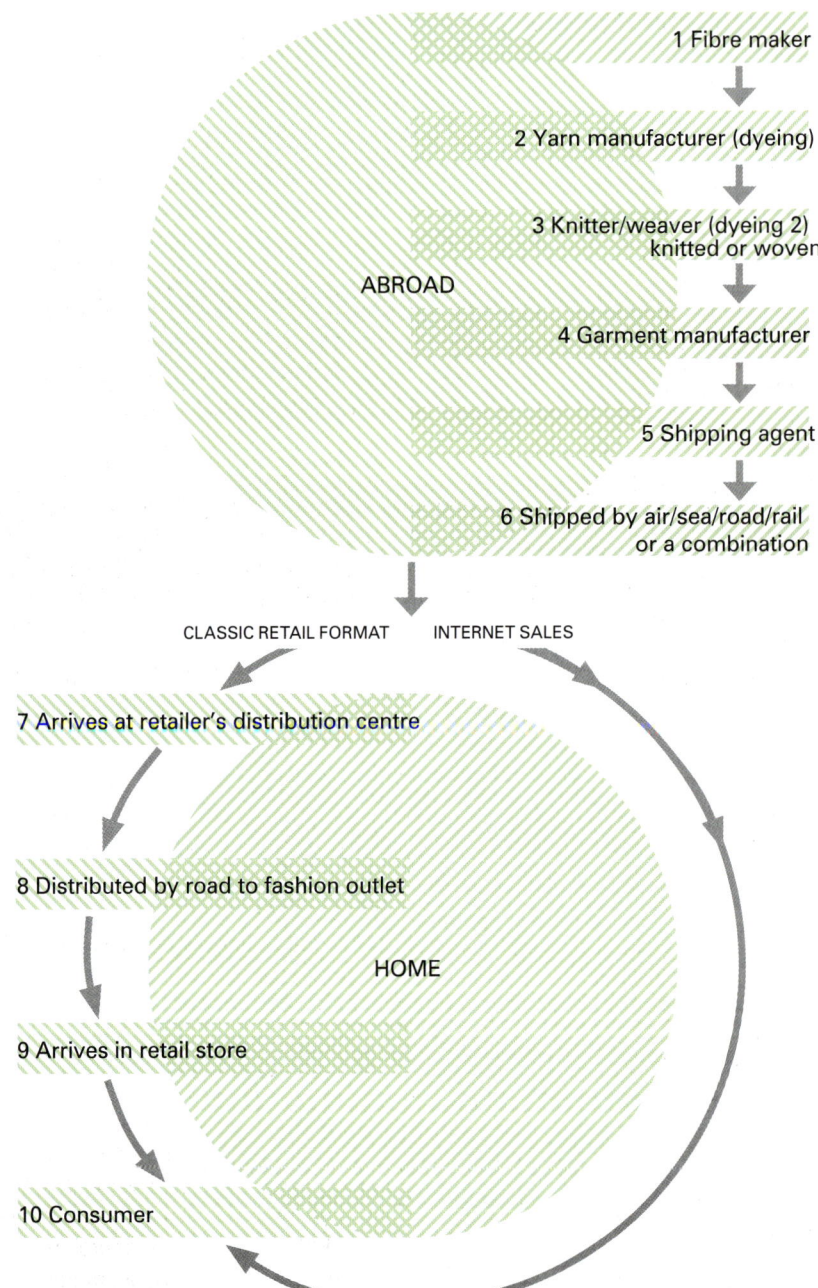

Figure 3.22 The fashion garment supply chain.
This diagram illustrates the supply chain for classic retail sales and e-commerce, showcasing the various stakeholders involved in the process from manufacturer to consumer.

of fashion and social trends and often due to marketing department demands. Manufacturers of yarns, fibres, and fabrics are under increased pressure to innovate to maintain competitive advantage, although the pace of change fluctuates significantly.

Fabric accounts for the highest proportion of the garment and can be up to 50 percent of the total cost. Buyers need to be mindful when choosing fabrics; not only do they need to be 'fit for purpose', they must align with the market level or selling price and the target cost price of the product range. It is important to consider the usable width and weight of the fabric when selecting and negotiating prices with suppliers. A narrow width is a challenge when lay planning and will increase the price and the percentage of wastage. Buyers should understand how to calculate the fabric consumption of a garment; this is so that they can understand the impact of fabric order minimums on purchase order minimums and re-buy quantities. Most fabric suppliers will look for a minimum order quantity of 1000 square metres to be able to guarantee the quality. The square meterage of fabric varies dramatically by garment (compare, for instance, the material needed for a bikini to that required to create a wedding dress with a full train). Buyers should engage in advanced preparation before attending fabric meetings, determining the fabric consumption for their specific product categories. This approach will enable them to establish the maximum and minimum price thresholds that they can feasibly pay per metre of fabric.

Production Lead Times

The lead-time is the time it takes from initial design idea to delivery to retail. The lead time will inform the merchandiser critical path (CP) and forms a crucial element to ensure the season's sales are achieved. There are several factors that affect fashion lead times in the fashion industry – the following are key:

The economy: the overall state of the economy where the garments are being consumed. A strong economy leads to increased demand resulting in factories being fully occupied.

Design and product development: the time needed to develop a design and create a pattern for a garment to be able to develop a product will vary depending on the complexity and technicality of the design and customization required.

Material sourcing: seasonal availability, technicality, minimum order quantities, and the shipping time can impact the lead times for sourcing raw materials, fabric, trims, and accessories.

Order volume: larger order volumes can require more time for production; even though they come with stability at the time, the factory may need to hire additional staff or invest in new equipment to meet the demand.

Quality control: an important use of time to ensure that the final product meets the required quality standards; however, the inspection and testing of materials and finished goods for quality can add time to the production process.

Supply chain logistics: the time it takes to transport materials and finished goods can affect production lead times, especially if the supply chain involves international shipping or customs clearance.

Communication: effective communication between different stakeholders involved in the fashion supply chain can reduce lead times; poor communication can lead to delays and missed deadlines. Innovation in communication technologies has made it easier to share information, collaborate, and track progress in real-time. Digital platforms such as PLM and ERP (enterprise resource planning) can help streamline communication and collaboration between different stakeholders, leading to more efficient production processes and shorter lead times.

It is important for the buyer to stay abreast of all new technological developments. Weaving looms and knitting machines are getting faster and can weave and knit increasingly intricate designs and patterns.

Figures 3.23–3.24 Changing technology – high tech 3D knitting machines have the ability to make full garments with limited human intervention.

In fact we are now able to programme knitting machines to produce finished garments with minimal or no sewing required, leading to greater efficiency and cost savings.

Shima Seiki from Japan, **Stoll** from Germany, and **Santoni** from Italy are all manufacturers of knitting machines that can knit entire garments without seams; their whole garment knitting technology allows for the production of garments and trainers with a three-dimensional shape and a customized fit.

Selecting and buying garments

Following the confirmation of fabric, the buyer will begin selecting and buying the garments that are to be included in the final range. The buyer will not make these decisions in isolation and they will work closely with the design team, finance, planning, and merchandising before seeking final approval or 'sign off' from the senior management. In most cases, except for small businesses, the buyer must obtain the consent of senior buying or board-level management for their final range selection.

Working to a predetermined buying plan, stating the numbers of brands, styles, colours, and sizes, the buyer will whittle down their initial wider range plan into a final, narrower collection. The final range plan must be balanced in terms of product categories, prices, and materials, to ensure that each garment will be profitable and desirable to customers. A balanced range plan may include a combination of core items, such as basics and essentials, as well as fashion-forward pieces that showcase the brand's creativity and innovation.

In Chapter 4, we will discuss the process of merchandise planning and explore the importance of getting the right mix for retail. We will examine the collaboration between buyers and merchandisers in ensuring a successful shift from the manufacturing stage to the retail space. This process takes place before, during, and after the initial communication and sourcing between suppliers and buyers.

CASE STUDY

The designer and buyer/merchandiser relationship: Stephen Park & Stephanie Stumbaugh discuss their perspectives

Stephen is an experienced graphic designer who specializes in licensing consumer products and captivating storytelling. With a diverse skillset as a multidisciplinary designer, he effectively brings brands and projects to life through powerful visual narratives.

Originally from the United Kingdom, Stephen began his career in graphic design at Runshaw college and successfully gained his BA(Hons) Graphic Design at Blackpool and the Fylde College of Arts. Stephen secured his first role as junior graphic designer at Basebuy Ltd and progressed to retail giant Matalan as menswear graphic designer. In 2007, after successfully securing a role at Abercrombie & Fitch, Stephen moved to the United States, taking the role of associate graphic designer. In 2014 Stephen moved to Gap Inc as Senior Design Manager-Graphics, utilizing his skills in product development, project management, fashion design, and graphic design, and in 2018 he moved to Old Navy Licencing department as senior manager for consumer products and creative merchandising. Stephen is currently a freelance graphic designer engaged in a number of exciting projects with Old Navy,

Figures 3.25–3.26 Stephen Park & Stephanie Stumbaugh

Dickies, Levis, Juro Miru, Dockers, Abercrombie & Fitch, and Abercrombie Kids. We met up to discuss the designer and buyer roles in the United States.

Stephanie Stumbaugh is a strategic buyer and senior merchandiser for both menswear and womenswear product categories with skills in knit, fleece, graphics, footwear, and accessories. Results-focused Stephanie is responsible for strategic vision and product planning in a competitive and consumer-focused environment.

Stephanie graduated with a BSc in Business Studies, specializing in retailing and consumer sciences. In 2011 she launched her career in the fashion industry through the Gap Inc retail management programme. In 2013, Stephanie took a leap to Old Navy, where she began as an assistant merchandiser and steadily climbed the ranks to become a senior merchandiser, overseeing women's shoes and accessories. In 2019, Stephanie pursued a new opportunity at Everlane, as merchandise manager, responsible for retail and womenswear. Following her successful tenure at Everlane, she then joined American Giant in 2022, continuing as a merchandise manager. Throughout her journey, Stephanie has demonstrated her expertise and passion for the fashion trade, making significant strides in her career.

Q: What is the structure of buying/supply and design teams in US fashion brands where you have worked and how do they work?

The merchandising/buying teams balance the art and science of creating a compelling assortment for the customer, acting as the liaison between the design team's new ideas and the business revenue. Design teams are responsible for providing trend forecasts and bringing new ideas to the table, while merchandising/buying teams are responsible for a comprehensive hindsight of what happened last year (what styles were strong and should be brought back, and what styles to exit for the upcoming season to make room for new ideas). Every product meeting should have a good amount of creative tension between merchandising/buying teams and design teams. If merchandising/buying is left to sole decision making, odds are the product assortment will look too much like last year and lack compelling new reasons for the customer to buy. If the design team is left to sole decision making, odds are there may be known revenue-driving styles that may be left out for unknown and unproven new ideas. Both for Abercrombie & Fitch and Gap Inc (Old Navy) the companies and daily structure were both heavily merchandising (buying) led. Each company had a specific focus on the buying side and less so on the design creativity. The key leaders and decision makers were merchandising led, reporting to the senior vice president (SVP) of buying and CEO. In both examples it is evident that it was a 60/40 or even a 70/30 buyer-led business. There is a typical structure in the traditional buying offices in the United States, each requiring a team in design and buying. For example, if we were considering the men's knits division there would be a buying team which included the merchandising director who would be in charge of the men's division, supported by the department merchandising manager (DMM) and the merchandising assistants (MAs). In the design section the design director would be in charge of the graphic design supported by the senior graphic designers and associate graphic designers. Generally, the larger the company size/revenue is, the heavier hand merchandising/buying has in the decision making, as that team is the owner of the financial performance at the end of the day. In the smaller companies and start-up companies who are relatively new and have limited historical data, the more willing they are to take risks and let design have a heavier hand in the assortment and decision making.

Q: How would you describe the collaboration and communication process between the fashion designer and the buying/supply professionals?

A healthy and collaborative relationship between design and merchandising/buying should have constant communication on an almost daily basis. There should be free-flowing conversations around what each person is seeing out in the market, what new ideas could benefit the business, and what current styles in the business are working/not working. Usually, merchandising/buying teams are looking at more direct competition/similar price point high street competitors for ideas, while the design team is looking at more aspirational and runway brands, so sharing ideas isn't duplicative and there is a well-rounded idea of the competitive landscape and opportunities. Merchandising/buying is also reporting out on business performance once a week (usually on Mondays), where they share with their design counterpart current trends in sales, down to what silhouettes are beating or missing forecast.

Q: Have you worked in roles where the buying/supply team are involved in the design process, and what kind of input do they provide? Who is primarily responsible for trend or product development – is this primarily the designer or do the buyer and designer work together?

In an average season the merchandising directors will take the concepts from the concept team and digest the seasonal needs. Then the seasonal needs would be aligned with the directors who would then map out the seasonal milestones and deliverables. As a buying team most of the buying direction would be communicated with the seasonal needs so the graphic department knows the volume of work ahead; for example, if a retailer or buyer gets feedback that 'Bold single-colour graphics are selling really well so we need to protect X per cent of newness within this bucket'. The weekly sales results will be communicated with the graphics team in order to leverage live data and selling trends. This could of course correct the original forecast and change the estimate of product sold.

From a buyer's perspective a standard season product pipeline contains the following flow of meetings for the preseason design process:

1 **Competitive shopping trips (owner: design).** Design goes out into the marketplace to buy samples for inspiration for the upcoming season. This trip should focus on new ideas to incorporate, as well as new and innovative ways to update current styles in the business that are best sellers (for example, new fabrics to cut best-selling silhouettes in).

2 **Concept/trend (owner: design).** An overall concept for the season is laid out (for example, '90s Nostalgia'), with key new pieces the design team strongly believes in that should be big ideas for the season based on their competitive shopping and trend research (for example, light wash jeans, baby tees, etc.). This is also where the design team comes with a point of view on the colour palette for the season.

3 **Hindsight (owner: merchandising/buying).** A comprehensive look at how the past season actualized from a financial point of view, from a gender, department, category, subcategory, and attribute level. If we take a men's bottoms business as an example, this hindsight should show:

   a. Gender: total men's business performance

   b. Department: men's bottoms vs the other categories in men's (did it overperform, underperform)

   c. Category: denim vs woven vs knit bottoms performance

   d. Subcategory: pants vs shorts performance

   e. Attributes: leg shape (straight vs skinny vs wide leg, etc), leg opening (elastic bottom vs open bottom vs jogger, etc), inseam length (cropped vs tall vs standard), fabrication (linen vs poplin, etc), colour (neutrals vs cools vs warms).

4. **Roadmap (owner: merchandising/buying).** Based on the hindsight, the merchandising/buying teams will create a roadmap or skeleton of an assortment that provides guardrails to design on upcoming product development needs. This should include total number of styles needed for the season, what styles to repeat and build upon, and slots for new ideas. The new ideas should have guardrails based on the hindsight and what the customer was gravitating towards (for example, if last year there were ten shorts styles that didn't drive the revenue needed, this year's roadmap might ask for only eight styles and limited new development, and explicitly ask for more ideas in pants).

5. **Sketch review/alignment (owner: collaboration between design and merchandising/buying).** This meeting is where the two teams align on the new ideas the design team is pitching in line with the roadmap asks. Design should push for new key ideas from the concept and from marketplace research, and merchandising/buying should feel covered from a business perspective that the new ideas fit into the roadmap asks. This is where the hard conversations may happen to balance the business needs and trends (in the above example, if the roadmap only had eight shorts styles slotted, but design is seeing shorts as a huge opportunity and an area of high development, the two teams will need to align on the best path forward for the trend and for the business). The outcome of this meeting is the alignment on all new styles to develop for the upcoming season, and those designs are sent out to vendors to create a prototype.

Q: What kind of market research or trend analysis does the buying/supply team provide to the design team to support their product development?

The merchandising/buying teams do competitive research and trend analysis, usually with a focus on direct competition/similar price point companies, while the design team is more focused on aspirational brands and runway shows. The merchandising/buying teams usually provide information around price points, visual presentations, and colour palettes seen in the direct marketplace (for example in a women's knitwear business, the merchandising/buying team would provide information like 'our biggest competitor is standing for sweater vests in a big way with a whole entry table dedicated to them, all at a $50 price point, in a range of bright and vibrant hues'). This

SELECTING AND BUYING GARMENTS

information can be added to what the design team is seeing out there from their trend work, and hopefully align on what they're seeing in the marketplace.

The design teams take inspiration/shopping trips to New York, Europe, and Japan to shop for key items that we could create new styles from. On return from these trips, the design and merchandising teams would meet regarding trends/costing and thoughts and, from their research, propose content. In Old Navy a lot came down to cost, a lot of content was loved in the initial design phases but, once planning and production were involved, the bulk of content ended up stripped back. In the licensing world the merchandisers would listen to the vendors and studios on how certain properties were performing in other retailers. Additional services such as WGSN and Style Sight were also leveraged by design to back ideas.

Q: How does the buyer or supply team influence the design decisions, such as colour palettes, fabric choices, or overall product assortment?
Design has the main say in colour and fabric choice, the only catch would be if a certain colour or fabric had performed poorly in the past. Regardless of upcoming trends, the buying teams would buy these with caution or smaller unit buys. The overall product assortment is ultimately a collaboration between both teams, as outlined in the standard season product pipeline flow of meetings for preseason design process (above). Depending on the company, if there is a stalemate in alignment and the teams don't agree, merchandising/buying usually has the final say in larger scale companies, where design may have the final say at smaller/start-up companies.

Q: How do the teams (both buyers and designers) stay updated on emerging product developments?
Design usually has a focus on:

1   Marketplace shopping at aspirational brands

2   Runway shows

3   WGSN or any trend forecast websites.

At both Abercrombie and Gap there is a dedicated concept team that sends out key trends and catwalk reviews, knowing that some shows and trends might be a year ahead for our customer. Additionally, in some areas, like my previous role in licensing, as the graphic designer I was the most important person for keeping people informed with trends and emerging market I.P. As a designer I developed a relationship directly with the licence vendors (who supply our competitors with content and the studios themselves). I would create a weekly email report with new market news from gaming charts to the movies' release dates.

Merchandising/buying usually has a focus on:

1. Direct competition/similar price point companies – shop online and brick-and-mortar. What are they standing for in a big way vs a smaller/test way, what silhouettes and fabrics do they have, what price points can they achieve and are those comparable to quotes we're getting from vendors for similar items, etc.?

2. Instagram/socials follow direct competition/similar price point companies to stay up to date with their big marketing campaigns, new launches, etc. Also, be sure to check your own company's tagged photos on Instagram so you can truly see who your customer is, how they're styling your pieces in real life, any common themes, etc.

3. Store visits to your own company – ask store managers what customers are asking for that aren't currently offered, what are the common themes in feedback from fitting rooms, etc.

Q: What role does the designer play in the decision-making process when it comes to selecting fabrics, colours, and materials for collections – does the buyer/supply team have any influence?

Like we discussed earlier, the design team has more of a say with fabrics and colours, but with everything it comes down to cost. The design team will work with the fabric research and development team to obtain brand affordable fabrics and materials for the season at hand. The merchandising/buying teams will provide design with the previous season's financial performance down to the fabric and colour level. This information should be in the back of the design team's mind as they're shopping and kicking off a new season to ensure new ideas have a good chance of driving revenue for the business. If the merchandising/buying team's hindsight lilac was a very tough colour last year, design may want to rethink the new shade of purple they want to stand for in a big way. Alternatively, merchandising/buying may need to be open to the shifting trends and identify that maybe last year was too early for our customer to be open to lilac, but now, after seeing it in a bigger way in direct competition, the customer may be more open to it this coming season. At the end of the day, collaboration and communication is key to having a balanced and profitable assortment!

Q: Do you have any advice for buyers of the future in terms of the future of the fashion industry?
From a designer's perspective, I would say America is very different to the United Kingdom, I could be creative with fifteen years of experience, but I would still find myself being told what to do by a buyer with two years of experience. The American buyers are super focused on business. Having a voice, moving up the ranks quick and fast, I've found that the toughest thing with the buyer/design relationship is trust. I trust the buyer who knows the numbers to use the money in the right way and rarely challenge financials unless I have data to sway the outcome, but 80 per cent of American buyers think they are designers. Communication, building rapport is critical, become the best buyer that can support the designer, and the designer should be the best designer to support the buyer. Merchandising would then give a planning outlook.

From the buyer's perspective, objectivity is king – never use the word 'I' in a meeting and always have your customer top of mind. 'I think this will do well', or 'I like this because' will be your downfall! Rephrase that to 'The customer will like this because'. At the end of the day, you are an advocate for your customer, so your own point of view should be on the backburner. If possible, start your career in a product category that you personally don't wear/purchase to teach yourself how to be objective and lean on sales data, marketplace research, and trend analysis to make decisions instead of your own personal opinions muddying decisions.

Chapter 3 summary

In this section, we delved into the buyer–supplier relationship and explored the key players involved in the supply chain responsible for the final range's selection and design. The chapter covered the buyer's research and communication strategies, emphasizing the importance of the relationship between the buyer, designer, and quality assurance team. It also touched on sourcing issues such as global sourcing areas, technology, and sustainability, highlighting the advantages of operating in a competitive global market. Furthermore, we discussed critical aspects of product selection, including textile science and product development, and the buyer's specific role in this process. By doing so, we aimed to provide a deeper understanding of the meticulous work and attention to detail required for successful seasonal purchases.

Questions and discussion points

After learning about the process of product sourcing aimed at crafting an ideal offering for customers, reflect on it from your own viewpoint as a consumer:

1. Which fashion retail outlet or fashion brand that you regularly shop for yourself provides the best overall product offer?
2. What aspect(s) of that retail outlet's range(s) make this offer so good?
3. When you go shopping for your own clothes, what are the most important attributes of a fashion range that you most look for?
4. Look at a selection of products across the store, including different categories, i.e. knitwear, jersey, denim, formal, dresses, and lingerie. Find the fibre content label, note the fibre content, and then note the country of origin. From this research you can start to identify sourcing regions for both fibre and product type.
5. Repeat activity 4 in a premium/designer store to see the differences or similarities of sourcing regions against cost and quality.
6. Undertake an audit of your own wardrobe and list all the different garments that you own. Once you have done this, analyse this list in terms of the number of garments per category, the number of different fabrics, and the number of different colours and country of origin.

Reflect on the answers you have given in questions 1–6 with reference to this task.

Exercises

As buyers undertake regular competitive shopping trips, they need to develop objective observational skills about the commerciality of competitors' ranges that will help them (and management) to develop the next season's range.

Working individually or as a group, visit two local fashion outlets (retailer A and retailer B). Answer the questions below as you browse around each outlet (you may need to make several visits).

Write up notes outside and not as you examine the stock – retailers may be sensitive about researchers working openly in their stores, so don't make it too obvious.

1 In each of your outlets, select one department (e.g. dresses, tops, jeans), then carefully go through the lines stocked and answer the following:

- How many different individual styles are displayed on the shop floor in your chosen department?
- What size ranges are being stocked in both? Do they vary?
- Do they have at least one size of every colour available on the shop floor? If not, try to estimate what percentage of size and colour options are unavailable to customers.
- How many different colours or prints are on offer in each department?
- Do they have the country of origin on the internal label – list the type of product and the country in which it was made.

2 Having visited the two outlets to have a detailed look at one product department in each, prepare a ten-minute verbal presentation aimed at a buying manager, then answer the following questions (comparing retailer A with retailer B's chosen product department):

- Which has the wider product offer and by how much; for example, how many individual lines or styles are displayed?
- Compare the size range stocked by each – comment on which has the widest size offer.
- Compare both departments as to which has a greater depth of stock: which stocks the most units of any one individual size and colourway?
- Which of the two departments has the most 'balanced' offer?
- What were the sourcing strategies of each department?

Figures 4.1–4.3 'Le Chouchou'. Jacquemus's Fashion Show 23/24. Fashion show with a difference where the front row guests take to row boats on the Grand Canal at Versailles.

Range and Merchandise Planning

4

Merchandising is a strategic function that not only improves the customer experience by offering visually appealing products but also plays a crucial role in driving sales and profitability. In many companies, the merchandising function is represented by the senior management team, reflecting its significance in the overall business strategy.

In this chapter, we will examine the close relationship between the fashion buyer and the fashion merchandiser, and we will put the complex process of merchandise planning into context. Merchandising here relates to the numerical and logistical planning that brings products from the manufacturer to the retail environment; this process relies on meticulous advanced research and planning.

Solid fashion buying and merchandising practices are essential to maximize profitability, so fashion buyers in turn have their business performance measured using key performance indicators (KPIs), which are driven by the business's overall financial objectives. Getting the right product and achieving the sales and stock plan is therefore crucial for all fashion businesses.

What is merchandise planning?

Fashion merchandising is a very broad concept that involves the process of selecting, allocating, approving, shipping, displaying, and selling fashion products to target consumers. Working closely with the design, buying, and sales teams, merchandisers analyse consumer and societal trends that inform the demand forecast. They must ensure that the product is in the right place at the right time for the right price in the right quantity and the right quality. They are responsible for identifying opportunities for growth that inform buying decisions.

The merchandise planning function plays a crucial role in predicting and controlling inventory levels that align with the sales targets of a season or period. At the same time, the merchandiser must understand the wants and needs of consumers, through the analysis and interpretation of market trends and consumer behaviour, to identify growth opportunities. The goal is to develop a merchandising strategy that accurately satisfies customer demands, boosts sales, and optimizes profits. Merchandising is challenging due to various factors, with stock control being the most significant. Insufficient stock can lead to lost sales, while overstocking wastes buying budget. Core responsibilities include opening and closing stock levels, price alterations, and the open-to-buy budget which manages re-buys and replenishment of existing and new product lines. Merchandisers will plan to avoid at all costs a 'dead stock' situation, which results in stock being sold at drastically lower prices. They will do this by ensuring that they turn the stock in line with the inventory period. Stock turn or inventory turnover is used to measure the efficiency of a fashion business's inventory management. It refers to the number of times that a company's entire inventory is sold and replaced within a given period, usually a season. A high stock turn indicates quick and efficient sales which maximizes profitability. On the other hand, a low stock turn suggests that a company is carrying too much stock, which can lead to lost sales and reduced profitability.

Most fashion companies have a range of products that are considered 'never out of stock' (NOOS). These products, which usually consist of basic items, remain relatively unchanged from season to season and can be easily integrated into future range plans with minor updates such as colour or fabric variations to keep them current.

The Complexity of Fashion Buying

Fashion is one of the most complex consumer products to buy, for the following reasons:

Unpredictability
Fashions and trends change rapidly and frequently, product that does not sell will have to go into sale at reduced price, leaving businesses with excess unsellable stock that reduces overall profitability.

Seasonality
Seasons require different types and weights of fabric and clothing type; the weather is extremely unpredictable, with rapid changes of product demand. Getting the right level of supply is often a problem.

Product complexity
There are so many different types of garments available to men, women, and children. Outerwear, underwear, formal, and casual clothing, combined with size and colour options, create literally thousands of individual stock-keeping units (SKUs).

Figure 4.4 Merchandisers are multi-skilled individuals and must keep on top of trends and the financial implications of a fast paced environment where the success of the sales relies on the choices they make.

The buyer–merchandiser relationship

There are many merchandising roles in the fashion industry – the role will differ from company to company. Fashion **retail** merchandising requires high levels of numeracy and data analysis to successfully regulate the planning, monitoring, and controlling of the proposed purchases and inventory management.

The **import** merchandiser is responsible for the planning, sourcing, purchasing, and managing of the delivery of fashion products from local or international suppliers to meet the demands of a retail or wholesale business. They will manage the critical path (CP) or use a product lifecycle management system (PLM) to coordinate with suppliers a timely delivery of goods, whilst negotiating prices and managing the logistics of importing goods. The goal of the import merchandiser is to ensure that the product is approved as per the CP and to optimize inventory levels to ensure that the right products are available in the right quantities to meet consumer demand while also maximizing profit margins for the business.

Visual merchandising, on the other hand, is where an individual works to create a conducive environment that will entice consumers to purchase goods through strategic product placement and visual displays, both in store and online.

Working together, the buyer and merchandiser typically hold similar levels of managerial authority. They usually work very closely together to ensure that their buying team (usually a one-product department) achieves their specific KPIs – a set of well-defined financial objectives required of each buying department for that season.

During the process of planning new ranges or evaluating trading performance, it is usual for the buyer and merchandiser to discuss jointly with the senior management team. Skilled buyers exhibit a high degree of numerical proficiency, enabling them to make informed decisions in relation to the operational and planning aspects of the merchandising function.

At the start of a new season, the buyers and merchandisers are effectively controlling and buying three seasons of stock:

- Last season – clearing and marking down slow lines
- Current season – delivering, monitoring, and reacting to sales by buying more or less product
- Future season – planning samples, writing orders, and planning delivery phasing.

The need for buyers and merchandisers to be very disciplined, organized, and responsive is obvious from the complexity of this task, not least because they will eventually be measured on their performance by the KPIs, as laid down by senior management.

The buyer's instinct vs planning

The successful buyer will make decisions based on both instinct and strategic data-informed planning.

Buying instinct refers to the ability to assess a trend or fashion development, identify opportunities and potential risks, and make decisions that will lead to success quickly and accurately. Instinct in buying is developed through time, experience, industry knowledge, and observation; it can be particularly useful in situations where there is limited time or information available, and in situations where the environment is rapidly changing, and decisions need to be made quickly to stay ahead of the competition. In contrast, planning requires analysis of sales data, market trends, and customer feedback to make informed buying decisions. Both planning and instinct are crucial for success, as a fashion buyer's well-honed instinct can help spot emerging trends and make quick decisions, while careful planning can ensure that the right products are available at the right time. Finding the right balance is important since over-reliance on instinct can lead to poor buying decisions, while excessive planning can limit creativity and hinder the ability to respond to unexpected trends or market changes.

Nonetheless, the global fashion industry is increasingly competitive, volatile, and dynamic, with markets constantly evolving at a rapid pace. Furthermore, consumers are becoming increasingly discerning, with heightened expectations for prompt delivery of their purchases. The challenge is compounded by consumers splintering into ever-smaller niche markets, placing further pressure on retailers to source precisely the right products.

The rapid advancement of technology and changing consumer buying habits have brought about a transformation in the high street. Consumers buy product through a multitude of channels to immediately get what they want, including social media, customer-to-customer (C2C) trading platforms, and the traditional shopping mall. Consumer and influencer feedback is becoming increasingly powerful in the fashion buying process, too, mainly as a result of personal communication technologies and the fast pace of data exchange. In response to the rapidly fluctuating consumer demand, the buying and merchandising planning process has evolved: the six-to-nine-month planning process is no longer a viable option for all products. Buyers and particularly merchandisers are reacting faster to changes in retail and consumer demand and adopting blended approaches to sourcing. The cost benefits of far-shore production require forward planning and time to ensure product reaches store for the selling period; however, a blended approach of dual sourcing near-shore and far-shore allows for faster responses to changing consumer demands. It comes with increased complexities – buyers are expected to meet more stringent standards than ever before, and their performance is monitored against KPIs.

How a buyer's success is judged

Fashion buyers are typically compensated fairly for their expertise and competence in identifying successful trends for the upcoming season. Although commonly referred to as 'having an eye' for identifying winning lines, it is important for young professionals to recognize the financial aspect of the job. Successful fashion buying requires sound financial management as a prerequisite for fun and creativity in the industry.

As mentioned earlier in this chapter, each product or category buying team will have a set of KPIs against which that team will be monitored and judged. If the buying team achieves their planned KPIs, then the business will make good profit and so thrive and survive. Most buying teams receive bonuses on top of their basic salary if they achieve a majority (or sometimes all) of their planned KPIs.

At the start of planning for a new season, the first step is to forecast the sales for the season; this will establish the turnover required to achieve strategic growth or development. The sales plan will identify the number of products needed in the range and the longevity of the selling period. The sales plan is followed by a profit plan which will set the target margin that the buyer will need to achieve for all products. Profit can loosely be described as the difference between the cost price from the factory and the price at which a garment is sold at wholesale or retail levels.

In general, last year's (LY) trading performance forms the basis against which a buying plan is created. Buyers will review trading performance and external factors that impacted the performance of a product line. From this they will identify how the range will move forward.

What you wear is how you present yourself to the world, especially today, when human contact is so quick. Fashion is instant language.

Miuccia Prada

Figure 4.5 Assorted markdowns.
When retail shops put out massive clearance racks, this could be a strong indicator that the forecast sales were incorrect or that a given trend ended before stock could be depleted.

KPI descriptors

There are many KPIs used to measure fashion business success; some of the most common KPIs used in fashion buying are described in Figures 4.6 to 4.9. There are other KPIs, but these are the most important that are required for overall fashion planning, control, and monitoring purposes:

The primary goal is to increase sales; buyers are given a sales target to meet or exceed, therefore they need to buy the **right product** to arrive at the **right time**, in the **right quantity,** and the **right quality**, sold in the **right place**.

It is important to have a keen eye on stock levels; too much stock ties up cash in the business and can lead to markdowns.

Even the best fashion businesses will have some slow lines. If stock is not selling at the expected rate, it is important to respond so that brands or businesses are not left with cash tied up in 'dead stock'. It is good practice for businesses to plan markdown each season.

Most of the buying KPIs are related to the product and the range, interaction with the consumer, and the sales environment. However, buyers also have strategic KPIs that influence all areas of the business.

Key performance indicators

As e-commerce continues to advance and with the use of various digital channels for shopping, retailers seek to focus on KPIs that are more specific to their websites. Here are a few KPIs that are distinctive to e-commerce:

Website traffic: a crucial KPI is the number of visitors. This can be tracked using web analytics tools like Google Analytics.

Conversion rate: the percentage of website visitors who complete a desired action, such as making a purchase.

Average order value (AOV): the average amount spent per order is an important KPI to measure retail profitability.

Customer lifetime value (CLV): calculates the total value a customer brings to your business over their lifetime.

Return rate: crucial KPI for measuring customer satisfaction and product quality, percentage of orders returned.

Abandoned cart rate: an important KPI to identify and address conversion difficulties is monitoring the percentage of customers who add items to their cart but leave before completing a purchase.

Customer acquisition cost (CAC): essential KPI to measure marketing and advertising impact.

New vs existing customers: how many patrons are new to the site vs how many have already visited.

Email marketing metrics: open rate, click-through rate, and conversion rate for email campaigns measure the effectiveness of your email marketing.

Social media metrics: follower growth, engagement rate, and click-through rate for social media campaigns are important KPIs.

Product affinity: categorizing consumers based on product preferences and/or purchases; specifically which products are purchased together.

Competitive pricing: pricing based on other e-tailer's retail prices, so as to provide competitive edge.

Planned Sales
- Sales forecast, determined by last year's sales and management projections, brands, retailers, and wholesalers looking to meet or exceed planned sales.

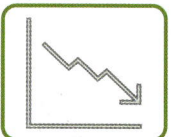
Actual Sales
- Actual money taken at retail at full price.
- Daily/weekly/monthly/seasonally/annually, compared to Last Year (LY) sales.

Sales or Gross Margin
- The difference between what the buyer pays and what all the stock is sold at, expressed as a total cash value and as a percentage.
- SM = revenue – cost of goods sold / revenue.
- Compares product categories to identify strong/weak performers.

Figure 4.6 Sales KPIs.

Stock Levels
- A valuation of stock in the business, expressed at full price retail value.
- Evaluated at end of day/week/season or year.
- Speed number of times stock is turned.

Stock Turn/Weeks Cover
- Efficiency ratio – the aim is to turn stock over quickly and acheive a high stock turn.
- 'This week's cover'/Sell through rate refers to the number of weeks that stock would last until it sold out.
- The fewer weeks of stock = the faster the stock turn (ST) = efficient buying and selling = higher profit.

Average Customer Spend/Units Per Transaction (UPT)
- The average amount a customer spends during each transaction within the store. This is derived by taking the total sales / the amount of customers who purchased and specified in a monetary unit.
- Retailers also look at units per transaction (UPT), or the average number of units sold to customers allowing them to better tailor their future marketing efforts.

Figure 4.7 Stock KPIs.

Markdown Level
- Markdown is expressed as a cash valuation (sometimes as a percentage) of the number of items marked down multiplied by how much they are reduced by. Occasionally, prices are marked up. For example, as manufacturing costs go up or currency exchange rates fluctuate.

Net Achieved Margin After Discount (NAMAD)
- The difference between the gross margin less the profit lost as a result of having to mark poor-selling stock down.
- 'Net buying margin.' This is the best indicator of a buyer's level of overall profitable buying success.
- Gross margin (GM) – profit lost (a negative loss) = **NAMAD**.

Deliveries on Time
- If the stock does not arrive on time sales will be lost due to no stock availability.
- Buyers will be measured on the number of shipments that arrive on time to maximize the selling period.

Figure 4.8 Profit KPIs.

Trend Forecasting
- Buyers must accurately forecast fashion and societal trends to make purchasing decisions that reflect the current market.
- Measured by the number of successful product launches, customer satisfaction, brand recognition and engagement.

Supplier Relationships
- Strong relationships with suppliers = buyer's success.
- Leads to better pricing, improved delivery times, and access to exclusive products.
- The quality of the relationship can be measured through feedback and supplier reviewing processes.

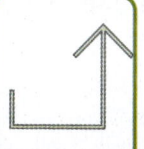
Returns
- Buyers must work on strategies to reduce the returns rate of their range.
- Minimize the issue of returns on stock levels.
- Minimize the cost of returns to business and environment.

Figure 4.9 Trend KPIs.

The merchandise planning process

Due to the pace of trend development and consumer demand, the fashion merchandising planning process is becoming more complex and challenging. Buyers and merchandisers need to be able to adapt and react at pace while also meeting sustainability and ethical standards, and embrace new technologies and production methods. The merchandise planning starts at 'top level' and will often feature within the business strategic plan for growth. This process will estimate how much merchandise will be sold, to establish a turnover target, which in turn will estimate how much needs to be purchased to produce an estimate buying budget.

As the industry has adapted to new trends and consumer preferences, the fashion seasons have changed and evolved from the two main trading seasons autumn(fall)/winter (early September–February) and spring/summer (March–August) to introduce additional seasons, such as pre-spring and resort, and in-season category updates or 'drops' which offer more opportunities for consumers to purchase product. To remain competitive some brands are beginning to showcase new ranges and collections off season to generate increased consumer interaction in pre-sale activity, intensifying demand. Buyers work closely with senior management to develop a sales plan for each season or period that aligns with forecasted turnover targets for specific selling periods. Using target margins set per product category, buyers then calculate their buying budget. The buyer and merchandiser will use historical sales data, along with insights from societal changes and market trends, to develop the retail sales plan and phasing. This plan will determine the number of

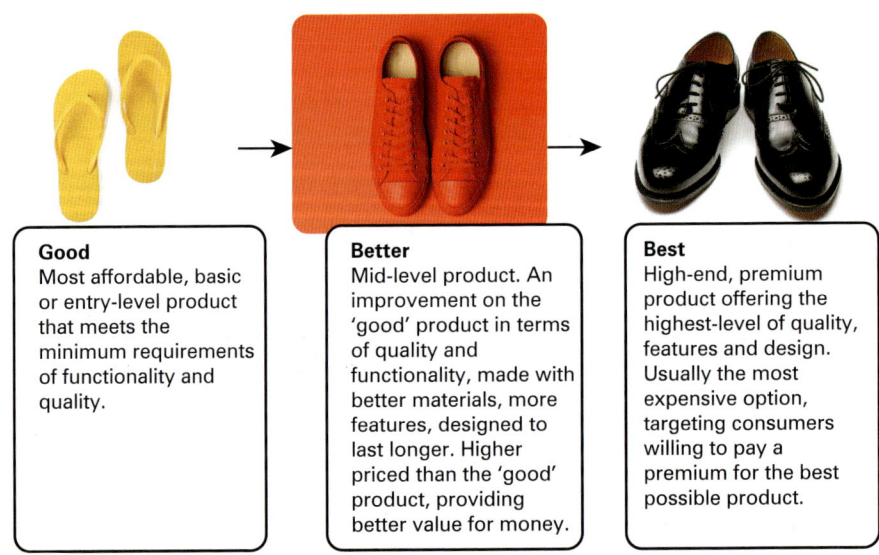

Good
Most affordable, basic or entry-level product that meets the minimum requirements of functionality and quality.

Better
Mid-level product. An improvement on the 'good' product in terms of quality and functionality, made with better materials, more features, designed to last longer. Higher priced than the 'good' product, providing better value for money.

Best
High-end, premium product offering the highest-level of quality, features and design. Usually the most expensive option, targeting consumers willing to pay a premium for the best possible product.

Figure 4.10 Good – Better – Best.
'Good – Better – Best' is a product strategy where buyers look at product options of varying quality and price to ensure they meet consumer needs and range plan diversity.

ranges, lines, sizes, and colours needed to achieve the targeted turnover and create a cohesive and logical range plan for retail or wholesale. The plan will include a delivery schedule into the business over the selling period or season by category, line, week, and in some instances colour, planning how the buying budget will be utilized to achieve the sales target.

To accommodate seasonal changes and allow for flexibility, buyers will set aside a buying allowance, known as 'open to buy' (OTB), which enables them to make in-season adjustments. A PLM system or purchasing database typically supports the planning process, providing a foundation for managing, controlling, and monitoring the entire supply chain from concept to consumer. Buyers and merchandisers typically review the results of the top-down sales plan with individual product buying and merchandising teams around fifteen months before the selling season begins. This enables product development and sourcing plans to commence. The planning process is based on overall retail selling value or prices, and the buyer and merchandiser collaborate to determine the percentage of each product category that should make up the plan. They then report back to the senior team with their recommendations.

Product Assortment Planning

To determine the range of products offered to customers in a particular season, buyers and merchandisers will use a product assortment planning process. They will analyse market trends, customer preferences, sales data, and other factors to create a customer-focused product mix that will maximize sales and profits.

The outcome is to create a well-balanced customer-focused range that optimizes inventory, identifying the number of styles, colours, and sizes, as well as the pricing and promotional strategy, and produce a timeline for product development, production, and delivery to retail.

Assortment considerations:

Brands: are you buying private labels or national brands? If both, what is the ratio of private labels to national brands? Which national brands will you add to the proposed range?

Size: based on your consumer market and target audience, which sizes will you order? Will you have extended sizes offered online?

Colour: consumer colour choices vary drastically, so keeping a varied assortment of both classic colours and seasonal trends is important. However, a buyer needs to determine the quantity of each colour to order to maintain consistent stock levels.

> **Textile:** choosing the right fabrics for the season is imperative (as discussed in Chapter 3). A buyer will look at trends as well as market climates to make these decisions.
>
> Buyers should be aware of previous seasons' sales, upcoming trends, and, most importantly, consumer needs when initiating the planning process.

Developing the initial seasonal buying plan

An initial buying plan provides the first breakdown of how the budget is about to be spent by category. Category descriptors vary by individual business but are generally self-explanatory. This initial breakdown into percentage of spend by category normally undergoes minor amendments as a result of problems, issues, events, and experiences until the 'buying point' is reached. A multitude of factors can change initial category plans, such as changing fashion, fabric, or garment trends, for example. Fashion buyers want to be as confident as possible when buying; the closer to the selling period they are, the more likely they are to be right.

Range planning

Whilst planning the budget, the buyer will need to evaluate the range to ensure it contains the correct product mix for the upcoming season or phase. In Chapter 2 we discussed the post-mortem report; this research will support the development of the final range. In most fashion businesses the range is split by classification, as shown in Figure 4.11. There are often four classifications: core staple products, semi-styled products, styled products, and fashion products. The range planning strategy is commonly attributed to Kotler's 1967 theory of analysis, planning and control.

Staple products refer to basic or core items that remain in production continuously, with minor alterations such as changes in colour or fit each season. Semi-styled products are also basics, but they have more variation from season to season in terms of cut, fabric, and colour. They have smaller production runs than core products. Styled products are a type of product with significant and frequent changes in design, cut, fabric, and colour from style to style. They also have shorter production runs than semi-styled products. Fashion products change abruptly with time, and production runs are crucial for speed to market. Fashion products have short production runs and frequent changes in design, cut, fabric, and colour.

The buyer and merchandiser will consider the current range of product sold. Reflecting on last year's sales performance and influencing factors

DEVELOPING THE INITIAL SEASONAL BUYING PLAN 123

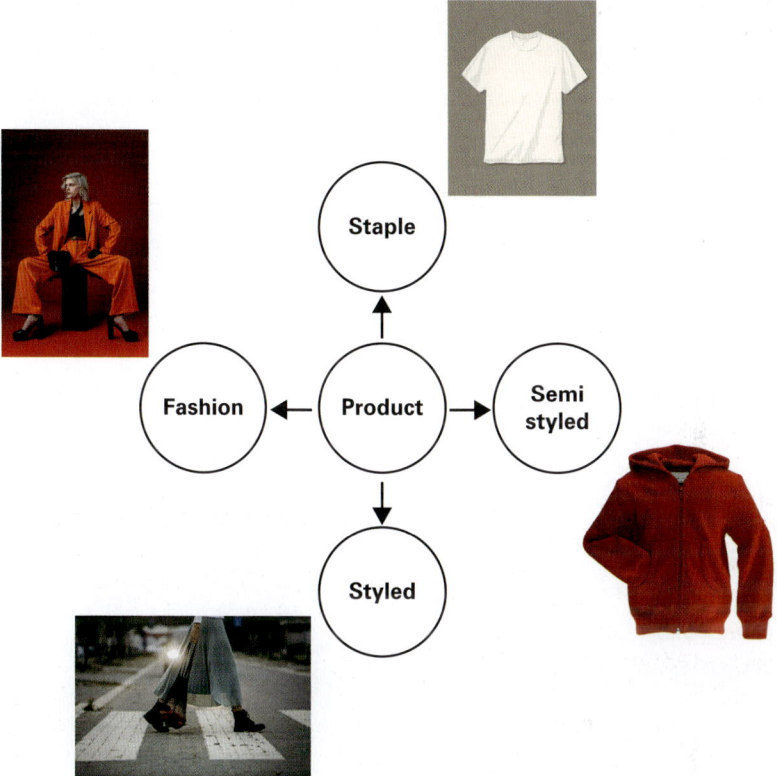

Figure 4.11 Range planning product classification.

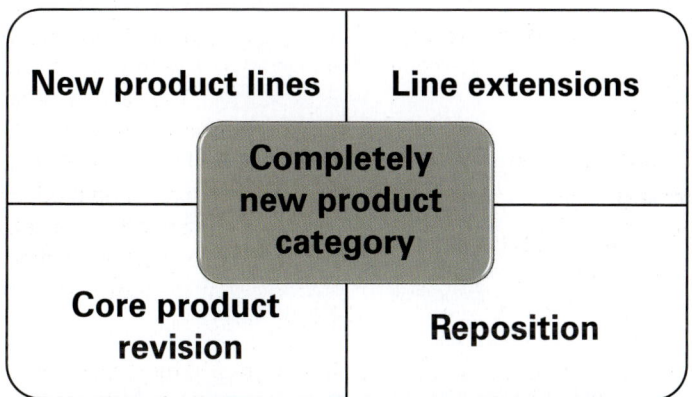

Figure 4.12 Range planning matrix.

they will identify how each product will move forward to the next season or phase, using the range planning matrix for each category (Figure 4.12).

Core product revision: moves a core product forward from season to season; this may include minor changes influenced by trends, looks, shapes, and silhouettes, e.g. round-neck T-shirt 24/25 with capped sleeves for amending to 25/26 roll sleeve.

Line extensions: enhancing product sales but remaining the same, e.g. jeans originally sold in regular length for 24/25, then for 25/26 introducing ankle grazers, short and long length, expanding the opportunity for sales of the same product.

Reposition: product with good sales in one category range can be repositioned to another category range, using the same resources without the need for redesign. Updating branding only, maximizing sales to the different target market.

New product lines: when a product reaches saturation, it needs to be replaced with an updated version. The product will remain in the same category and price slot but will be updated in line with consumer needs and trends.

Complete new product category: when a buyer sees a gap in the market and launches a new product category that will grow the range and enhance sales revenue. For example, if the brand does not sell formal wear, they may develop a concept range to test the market to grow season on season or keep it as a single seasonal drop.

Merchandise assortments

Buyers will thoroughly review sales reports to create the seasonal buying range, evaluating the total assortment of goods, or the merchandise classification, to determine product-specific needs that the company may invest in for the season or phase that will create the anticipated turnover. For example, going into the spring season from winter, buyers will begin to dramatically scale back on heavy outerwear, coats, to make way for lighter-weight tops and bottoms in preparation for changing climate conditions.

A buyer may also be introduced to new silhouettes or materials from the manufacturer, at which time they will have to decide what this merchandise should be classified as (i.e. knits, wovens, casualwear, or eveningwear, etc.). Sometimes, product assortment is determined by climate, location, trend, or a combination of these factors – this research is necessary to begin the forecasting process.

Forecasting sales and stock

In collaboration with key stakeholders in the sales and inventory teams the buyer will analyse previous season's sales data and evaluate the impact of new retail opportunities and customer feedback. This information will determine purchasing decisions for the next season's range. The analysis should delve into specifics on colour or size, or as broad as totalling sales for the entire classification of womenswear. These reports enable a buyer to forecast how each department will fare based on the targets set; at which time they are able to make the appropriate buys necessary to achieve these specific sales goals. As the buyer and merchandiser work to plan the seasonal range, these planning proposals will become more detailed and precise, allowing all members of the organization to see the intended buying direction.

Merchandise pricing

As mentioned previously, a buyer's job is more than product selection. They are tasked with working out the pricing strategies for each of those products purchased. Knowing this, a buyer must be well versed in mathematics, as any slight discrepancy in pricing could cause a loss of profit for the firm. Keep in mind that pricing varies based on variables such as firm size, type of goods being purchased, projected sales plans, and profit margin goals, etc., but the basic maths for determining retail sales price is fairly standardized.

Setting the retail price

Even though making a profit is key, it is important to consider the consumer when setting your retail pricing. Price is a way to select a target segment of the market. Price is a way to differentiate the offer. A high price can impact consumer values, a low price can be seen as a bargain, or perception of quality. Retail pricing is set using an initial markup for wholesale or ready-to-wear merchandise while target margin is used for own or branded product.

Retail/Wholesale pricing

The markup amount is the difference between the wholesale and retail prices. It is determined by utilizing the formula below:

Markup = selling (retail) price – cost of merchandise.

For example, if you bought one unit at $100.00 and charged the consumer $250.00 for it, the calculation is:

Markup = $250.00 (selling price) – $100.00 (cost of merchandise)

The overall markup dollar amount is $150.00, which is then converted to a percentage.

To determine the markup percentage, you must first determine whether there will be an individual markup or a cumulative markup. Individual markups are done on a specific item (such as men's Levi's 511 denim), whereas cumulative markups are done to an entire product category (i.e. all men's denim styles). Cumulative markup percentages are typically used for comparing merchandiser category performance against company sales projections, and both formulas are expressed as percentages. An example of an individual markup calculated is as follows:

Individual markup:

markup percent =[($250.00 (selling price) – ($100.00 (cost of merchandise))/ $250.00 (selling price)] × 100%

Or, as in our earlier example:

60% (markup percent) = [($250.00 (selling price) – ($100.00 (cost of merchandise))/$250.00 (selling price)] × 100%

Department	Actual sales $K Last year [LY] (Spring/Summer)	Planned sales $K This year [TY] (Spring/Summer)	% +/− TY vs. LY	Rationale for + or − growth
Dresses	150	200	+ 33.3%	Trend forecaster sees strong 50s style revival
Blouses	100	110	+ 10%	Formal shirts not very 'in'—move to casual look
Casual tops	200	250	+ 25%	Strong casual/easy fit look
Trousers	50	50	— (or flat to LY)	Formal trousers not strong at shows
Shirts	100	150	+ 50%	Miniskirt making a comeback
Jeans	150	200	+ 33.3%	Massive interest in branded jeans and washes forecast
Shorts	25	50	+ 100%	Shorts extremely strongly forecast
Swimwear	80	100	+ 25%	Hot summer forecast = exciting new prints
Lingerie / Underwear	100	105	+ 5%	Steady/static—no new product
Hosiery	40	35	− 12.5%	In decline—leg tanning more dominant trend
Accessories	80	100	+ 25%	Italian style handbags and sunglasses ever-popular
Grand total	$1075K	$1350K	+ 25.6% *	* denotes very strong overall planned growth for womenswear

Figure 4.13 Womenswear planning matrix.
A typical first planning proposal for womenswear spring/summer, showing the broad flow of the planning and buying process from initial plan to the start of the season. Note that due to the differing lead times of product types and levels of fast fashion product involved with individual fashion businesses, this diagram represents an approximation only.

What this translates to is that 40 per cent of the retail sales price of $250.00 is what the wholesale cost is, or 60 per cent of the retail price is profit ($150.00). Knowing this percentage allows retail buyers to compare past performance of similar/like goods and ensure they are generating enough revenue for overhead expenses associated with e-tailing and brick-and-mortar plants.

Own label or branded pricing

Buyers who work for own brands who sell direct to retail will be set a target margin to calculate their cost prices. The retail prices are set in line with the consumer expectations and maximum price levels. Once retail pricing is set, the target margin is applied to give the buyer the cost price target that they must achieve to make the forecast profit levels. The margin as a percentage is the difference between landed cost price and retail selling price. An example of margin calculation is as follows:

Retail sales price (RSP) $100.00 and target margin (TM) 65 per cent

Cost price = RSP × 1 minus the TM

Cost price = $100.00 × (1 − 0.65) or $100 × 0.35

Cost price = $35.00

Therefore, if an own or brand buyer wants to retail at $100 and they have been set a target margin of 65 per cent to achieve this margin they must purchase the product from the supplier at a landed price of $35.00 as shown in Figure 4.14.

Below are a few key terms to be familiar with when discussing merchandise pricing in a fashion buying office:

- Net sales – the cost of goods sold (gross margin – operating expenses = profit (or loss)) before taxes.
- Markup – the difference between the cost of the good (wholesale price) and its retail sales price.
- Markdown – a reduction in the original retail price of in-stock merchandise.
- Cost of goods sold – the cost of merchandise plus any transportation and/or work-related costs that incurred getting the goods from the seller to the retailer.
- Price point – a price range that has been established by the retailer for the price of their goods. Typically looked at as discount, budget, moderate, contemporary, better, bridge, designer, or haute couture.
- Open to buy (OTB) – a specific dollar amount left over in a season for a buyer to purchase with (Figure 4.15).

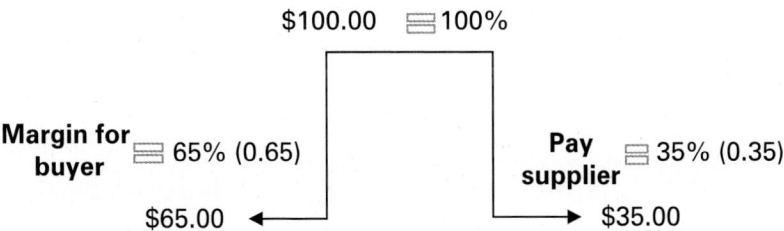

Figure 4.14 Retail price, cost price, and margin.

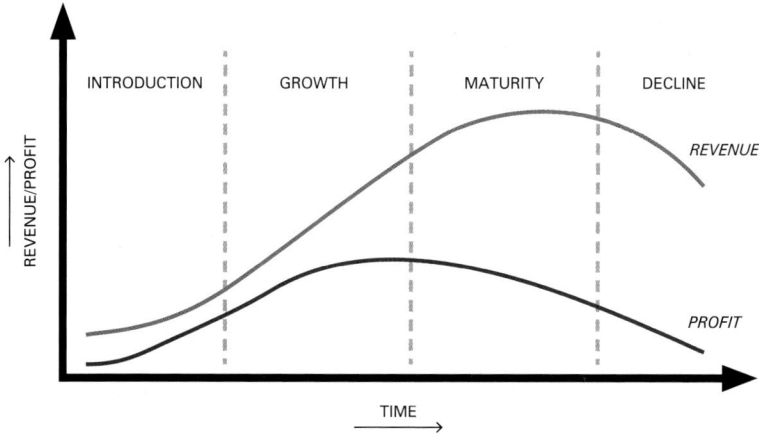

Figure 4.15 The product lifecycle.
The product lifecycle shows the upward and downward trajectory of a product based on how much money the product has made in relation to the time the product has been on the market. There are many economists who discuss product lifecycle theory. However it is often attributed to Philip Kotler's marketing management theory of 1967, the stages still remain relevant in today's markets.

Markdown pricing

Buyers will often take a risk on product selection; there will be times that this does not pay off and therefore there may be some products that do not fare so well throughout the selling period. These items end up as slow sellers due to issues such as failing trends, weather, quality, over assortment, and/or too much stock. Buyers take these variables into account and will conduct merchandise markdowns to drive sales and, hopefully, still achieve a profit for the season. Buyers must be well aware of the product lifecycle and make quick (but well-thought-out) decisions in their markdown strategy. Markdowns made too soon may result in a loss of potential profit, and markdowns taken too late lose their window of opportunity to clear inventory levels prior to next season's buys arriving. Note that markdowns can be temporary or permanent pricing strategies.

Markdowns are usually built into the overall retail price at the start of the season, with the intention of 'marking up to markdown'. While many retailers are hesitant to initiate markdowns, especially smaller establishments, it is a necessary tool to replace slower selling stock with new products for the season. Customers are fully in tune with merchandise at their favourite retailers, and a retailer risks losing repeat clientele if they don't often introduce new stock.

Retailers will either place goods on temporary or permanent markdowns. Temporary markdowns are done to stimulate slow sales or to drive interest in a particular product or brand and are often referred to as point of sale or promotional markdowns. On the other hand, permanent markdowns help to devalue product worth, thus providing monetary reprieve in terms of taxes and insurance at the end of the year. This is typically issued to product that is in the mature to declining stages of the product lifecycle.

Understanding why and how retail buyers markup or markdown their product is important because it puts the retailer at a stronger competitive edge and allows them to be proactive before and during the fashion buying season.

Risk and range planning

When planning a range, it is important to capture the trends of the given season; this may mean considering and including unusual prints and highlight 'risky' colours. In reality the majority of fashion customers err on the cautious side, not wanting to stand out from the crowd; however, the buyer must consider the risk factor of lost sales if the range is too bland. Good fashion buyers and merchandisers realize that their range needs these fashion elements, but tend to under-buy the extremes of fashion which, if left over at the end of the season, will require price reductions to clear stock levels, that may damage overall profitability.

Reducing levels of riskier merchandise

The fashion industry's press and social media tend to highlight the latest and most daring fashion trends. While experienced buyers exercise caution when investing in these extreme styles, even the most conservative buyers purchase some riskier fashion pieces to maintain a balanced range that presents the right overall impression to consumers. The idea of intentionally selling out of the more risky merchandise before the end of a season, commonly known as 'selling short', is a sound commercial strategy. While it may be difficult to convey this to those unfamiliar with the practice, it's always preferable to have excess inventory of classic colours like black, which have timeless appeal and can sell well into the following season, rather than risk being stuck with items in trendy but limited colours like neon fluorescent.

Getting the size balance right

Standardized sizing is not a new concept and has influenced fashion sales since the early twentieth century. In the 1940s through the International Organization for Standardization (ISO) the fashion industry developed a standard sizing system to support international trade. However, it wasn't until the 1970s that there was significant impact on international size standardization, when the ISO metric sizing system was introduced. Today, many countries have their own sizing standards that are tailored to their population. However, there is still a significant amount of variation in garment sizes between different retailers and brands, even when selling items that are labelled as the same size.

One of the most common reasons for a returned product is poor fit, especially when the purchase has been through an online platform. What customers most want from a range is for their size to be available and for a garment to fit well. Customers who can rely on a brand, shop, or range's consistency of fit will usually come back. Getting fit right and having sizes always available is a strong customer draw. This is especially so for jeans, shoes, intimates, and tailoring, where close body fit is an imperative. Good fashion buyers spend a great deal of time on getting fit right. Merchandisers spend even more time ensuring size availability. It is important for buyers and merchandisers to understand the size demographic of their consumer base and ensure they buy the correct sizes and correct quantities across the size mask. It is common for online young fashion labels to start with size zero to capture the youth market, in contrast to some older established brands who may start their size mask with an 8 or 10. In recent years there has been increased pressure for the fashion industry to address issues of size inclusivity and body diversity, which has led to changes in the way brands are marketing their products and the ambassadors that they choose.

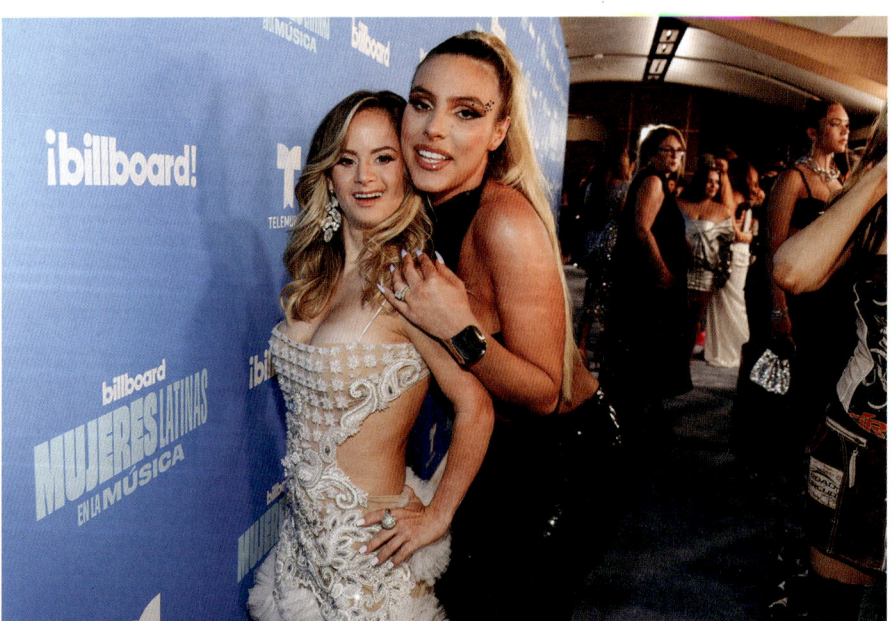

Figure 4.16 Sofía Jirau, the first Victoria's Secret model with Down's syndrome.

Range width and depth

During the planning process buyers will make decisions regarding the width and depth of the range, a concept that refers to two different aspects of the product offering; these decisions cannot be made in isolation and consideration must be made according to consumer demand, budget, and selling space.

Range width refers to the number of different product categories or styles included in the range. For example, a range might include dresses, tops, skirts, and trousers, indicating a wider range of product types.

On the other hand, depth refers to the variety of options within a particular product category or style. For example, a range might offer dresses in different lengths, styles, fabrics, and colours, indicating a deeper range of options within the dresses category.

Generally, a wider range with more product categories or styles is more likely to attract a larger customer base, while a deeper range with more options within each category leads to increased customer loyalty and repeat business. However, it's important to balance width and depth to ensure that the range is cohesive and meets the needs and preferences of the target customer base.

For traditional brick and mortar retailers, space is the main driver of range offer or range width; large department stores can offer thousands of individual fashion lines, whereas a small boutique may only carry a few hundred. However, with the rise of e-commerce platforms, the limitations of physical space have been eliminated, allowing retailers to expand their range width through multi- and omni-channel retail strategies. As a result, we are witnessing an increasing number of retailers offering a broader and more diverse selection of products.

Merchandisers will analyse sales data and consumer preferences to ensure that the correct numbers and sizes and colours are available to the consumer, especially when they are sold in store. While it may be a fashion ideal to stock all sizes and colours all the time, this is rarely feasible, and most fashion retailers are unable to offer 100 per cent availability for colours, sizes, or product lines. Nevertheless, many aim to achieve a 90 per cent availability rate, which is considered a key performance metric. To address the issue of out-of-stock items, retailers may offer customers next-day delivery to their home or to a store to prevent lost sales. This is sometimes referred to as a 'walk-away'. Additionally, retailers may provide other solutions, such as ordering the item through the company's website or contacting another store to locate the desired item.

Getting the range balance right

A key skill of any buyer is to ensure that when customers walk into one of their retail outlets, or browse online, they see product that immediately excites them and makes them want to look around, stop, try on, and hopefully … purchase something! Subconsciously, we make quick judgements as we walk past a shop window, walk through a department, or scroll on social media. Getting the range balance right is the secret to creating this instant appeal; and again, it is a skill that is highly developed in the best and most successful fashion buyers.

The main factors that influence range balance are:

- Price points: offer products at different price points to ensure you cater for different budgets. Each range should have a good mix of entry-level, mid-range, and premium priced products.
- Appropriate range width: a good mix of products across different categories; some brands divide their range into sub-categories like casual wear, formal wear, sportswear, etc. to cater to specific customer needs.
- Colours and designs: ensure the variety of colours and designs is in line with trends and preferences of the target customers, catering to different seasons, occasions, and regions.
- Sizes: to cater to customers with different body shapes and sizes, retailers or brands may also offer petite, tall, or plus-size ranges.
- Diverse selection of brands: especially important for branded merchandise retailers.
- Stock availability in all sizes, colours, designs, and fits – often the hardest goal to achieve.

Today's consumers are used to instant gratification, in terms of locating and buying fashion products immediately. They also expect endless choice and brand value. Fashion buyers and merchandisers know that if you fail to attract immediately and to provide the exact product by size and colour, most customers will look at competitors. It is vital that stock is available to purchase at all times and clear communication is made with the consumer about when the stock will be delivered. However, it is common practice for buyers to plan lines that might easily become satisfactory replacements for the customer if their first choice is not available. Fashion buyers work tirelessly to review option availability with their merchandisers. Perfection is never possible but buying a well-balanced range overall can greatly assist in switching consumers to another similar best-selling line in the range.

Figure 4.17 GREEDILOUS – Runway, Seoul Fashion Week SS 23.
AI-inspired collection, from designer Younhee Park the visionary behind GREEDILOUS, introducing a whole new dimension of possibilities by incorporating technology and the infinite Metaverse.

Selecting and grading the store ranges

The key drivers to when and how a range is bought depend upon whether the buyer is buying national- or private-label goods. Buying a national or branded label is normally done much closer to the start of the season, as the product design and factory negotiation processes have already been carried out by the brand; the buyer simply sub-selects from a range previously prepared for them.

Private-label buying is much more complex, with a longer lead time than for branded buying. However, with both methods it is still ultimately the buyer (in conjunction with the merchandiser) who must reduce the range down to one that is right for a given business and based on the negotiated time frame.

Buyers will always have more samples than they can possibly fit into their final range selection, as stores always have size limitations. Individual shops in a chain all have varying floor areas, thus limiting sales floor and back-stock space. Usually, businesses put similar-sized stores together into five to ten store groupings. Each buying and merchandising team will plan the exact number of lines that will go to all stores, with the widest or most complete range of lines going to the very large stores.

Merchandisers and buyers spend a great deal of time grading ranges in order of importance. Deciding on ranges for smaller shops is, in fact, the hardest job, as this small range will have to satisfy the majority of customers with a limited offer – a very difficult thing to achieve.

Product sampling and final range preparation

Gathering and refining samples and/or fabric and colour swatches is a continuous process during the range development process. Good buyers continually collect fabric ideas for colour, texture, and design inspiration, which can then be used when developing private label ranges. Most buyers keep working files of cuttings, pictures, drawings, and photographs that they feel may be useful, in a similar way to fashion designers. Samples are then presented at the final range meeting, usually using live models to show the product to its best advantage.

Preparation for the final range

Although management will have been involved during the preceding months, reviewing line and range developments during regular planning meetings, it is the final range meeting that is the most important. It is here that the whole buying team will be expected to support the buyer's range, in terms of design, quantities purchased, colour, size, and assortment balance. Whether buying private label or selecting from a new branded range, all decisions are then generally ratified by management at the final preseason range presentation.

The sampling sequence for private label products

In advance of the season buyers will often work with fabric manufacturers to arrange lab dips for the variety of fabric qualities that are going to be used for the final range. This is to ensure colour continuity is maintained across the colour pallet and fabric types.

The garment sampling process for own-label products varies slightly according to individual buying offices, but it generally has three distinct stages:

1. The fit sample. Often not actually manufactured in the final fabric, but it helps to develop and check the initial fit. Garments are usually made in a size 12 or medium and are tried out on the office's fit model. Any necessary alterations are then sent to the manufacturer to correct; the sample may go back and forth to the supplier a few times until a perfect fit is achieved.

2. The final approval pre-production sample. The final garment in the right colour and fabric is delivered in all sizes, all of which are checked against the originally agreed fit sample. Fabric will have already been sent away for testing prior to this, to check colour fastness, washing and dry-cleaning performance, light fastness, wear durability, and other product-specific tests, such as chlorine resistance for swimwear.

3. Production sample. As manufacturing starts, early production samples are usually express air-freighted to the buyer and checked against the final approval sample. Things like labels, swing tickets, and care instructions are also checked.

Branded approach to sampling

When buying from national brands or designer ranges, suppliers' samples are often in short supply, and the branded

Figure 4.18 Sacaï Men's Fall 2023 and Women's Pre-Fall 2023.
Chitose Abe, the creative director of Sacai, known for hybrid collections that are designed for longevity. A collaboration with Moncler and Carhartt, resulting in a unique blend of high-end fashion and utilitarian style.

buyer is often unable to retain samples. In this case, images of samples will be provided by the supplier or will be taken by the buying team to later remind them of the range. For final branded range presentations, the garments' ranges are borrowed for the day and later returned.

Managing samples

All samples, whether for private label or branded buying purposes, are valuable items. They cost a great deal to make and are often unique: it is therefore vital that they do not get lost. The care, labelling, tracking, and movement of samples is a major responsibility of the buying assistants. Sample rails and sample rooms need to be constantly tidied and rearranged, ensuring that samples can be quickly located.

Sealing samples

High end fashion houses and iconic brands incorporate the sealing of samples approach. This means placing a metal or plastic non-removable seal attached by a wire loop onto samples once they have been checked and accepted. The buying office will seal at least two samples (sometimes more), sending one back to the manufacturer and retaining one or more for themselves.

Sealing samples ensures that if any product, quality, sizing, technical, or other disputes arise, then both parties can refer back to these agreed samples to check what was ordered.

Promotional samples

As well as the flow of samples back and forth from buyer to suppliers, buying teams also have to contend with a fast and varied demand to loan samples out for other business-related purposes. These include the following:

- Internal and external press and fashion shows and events
- Photo shoots for shopping catalogues and visual merchandising purposes
- Photo shoots for advertising and PR
- Photographs for e-commerce sites.

The level and type of sample demand made upon individual buyers and their buying teams obviously depends on the type and size of the fashion business involved.

The final range presentation meeting is necessary for buyers to get total 'buy in' and agreement from the managers that the range represents the best selection of product for the targeted customer. This key meeting will probably also be attended by the in-house design team and QA team. Other attendees at a final range meeting might include the directors and/or heads of buying and merchandising. Often, the head of a company might also be present.

Presenting the final range

Presenting the final range can be a very stressful time for both buyer and merchandiser who will aim to 'work' the meeting together to confirm the rationale and logic of their range proposals. It is at times like these that a buyer's verbal communication skills are tested to the fullest, so both buyer and merchandiser need to be well prepared as they finally present the culmination of many months of planning work.

The merchandiser will have prepared highly detailed, numerically based planning sheets that clearly show the sizes, colours, delivery dates, store grades, and anticipated profit margins, as well as the percentage of the OTB (open to buy) that is to be spent on other product categories.

The size and proposed growth of each category in comparison to that achieved in the previous year will be examined, with the buyer justifying their products and range to all assembled.

Good buying and merchandising teams will probably have only minor alterations and suggestions made to them by management at the end of the presentation. These will be recorded and action-checked to ensure later follow-up by the buying and merchandising teams. If a buying team has previously had a difficult trading season, it is usual for management to spend more time ensuring that these past problems are not repeated.

Both the fashion buyer and merchandiser need to be confident in the final range presentation meeting in order to succeed. Uncertainty, lack of conviction, poorly researched facts, and weak rationale are no basis for company directors to sign off on the intended range.

In the next chapter, we will look at new trends in the buying industry that ultimately enable buyers to remain one step ahead of the retail game.

Buyers are concerned about how quickly inventory can convert to cash.

Linda Carter, President & Principal Consultant, Retail Management Advisors

CASE STUDY

WhichPLM, Mark Harrop – Expert Fashion Process & Technology Advisor

In the context of fashion buying, effective management of the product lifecycle is crucial. The use of product lifecycle management (PLM) software systems allows buyers and merchandisers to optimize their processes and resources. PLM systems oversee the entire lifespan of a product, from initial design to manufacturing, distribution, and eventual end of life. While the concept is not new and can be traced back to the 1980s with the introduction of computer-aided design (CAD), the focus shifted in the 1990s to include integration and collaboration between departments and wider stakeholders, resulting in the development software and PLM systems we see today.

With a proven track record in facilitating the digital transformation of fashion businesses worldwide, WhichPLM is the primary resource for brands, retailers, and manufacturers seeking to revamp their entire technology ecosystems. They offer advisory services that assist clients in selecting the most suitable PLM system to meet their specific needs. WhichPLM's strategic services are designed to drive fundamental improvements and focus on unlocking and enabling significant changes in the working practices of the fashion industry.

By assigning a monetary value to these benefits, they can assess whether an investment is accomplishing its intended objectives. The emphasis is on ensuring that the fashion industry understands 'how and what to measure' to fulfil Sustainable Return on Investment (SROI) goals and demonstrate that sustainability should now be considered a profit driver rather than a costly decision.

WhichPLM assist their clients and partners in comprehending the methods for evaluating the societal impact of an investment or project through the identification of SROI. The aim is to alleviate the concerns of retailers and brands regarding the global sustainability targets they are obligated to meet, and to empower brands, retailers, and their manufacturing partners at various tiers (1 to 6) to quantify the economic, social, environmental, and manufacturing advantages associated with investments.

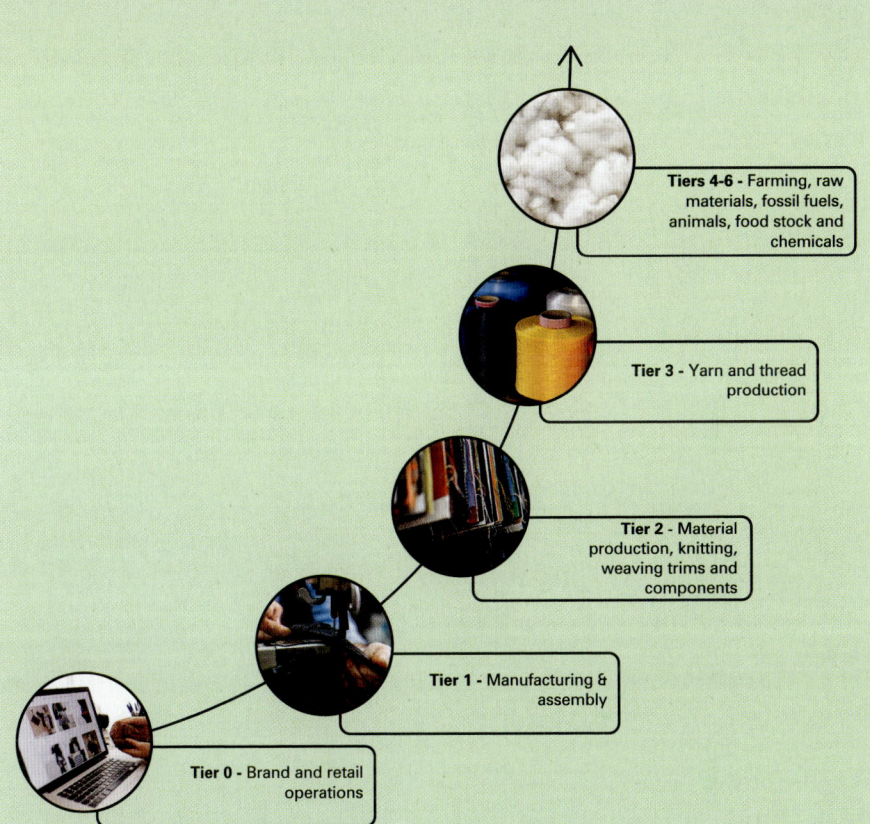

Figure 4.19 Product lifecycle management.
Working with all levels of the business, WhichPLM aid in the creation of a company's digital roadmap by formulating a vision, strategy, and practical requirements. Operating throughout the complete digital value chain, spanning from Tier 0 to Tier 6, WhichPLM promotes optimal practices for design, development, and manufacturing, while also addressing environmental concerns and supporting sustainability initiatives and all types of data.

Interview

Q: Who are WhichPLM and how do you operate within the fashion business sector?
Having accumulated fifty years of experience in fashion, Mark has been a first-hand witness to the digital transformation that has taken place in the global fashion industry. Reflecting on the past, Mark recalls that the initial steps towards digitization in the fashion industry began in the late 1970s with the introduction

Figure 4.20 Mark Harrop, WhichPLM.

of innovative payment and data capture systems. The mid-1980s saw the initial development of CAD, at the time a revolutionary concept. The foundations for PLM began in the 1990s through the ground-breaking business approach of collaborative product management (CPM), a set of practices that focused on involving cross-functional teams and stakeholders in the process of managing and developing a product throughout its lifecycle. Emphasizing collaboration, communication, and coordination among different departments. The industry wanted more and in 2003 CPM evolved into PLM – product lifecycle management – a radical move that provided a framework and technology-enabled approach for managing the entire lifecycle of a product, from ideation and design to manufacturing, distribution, and end-of-life. Following twenty years in corporate America, Mark established his own UK business in 2007. At this time the sales of PLM systems reached unprecedented levels and Mark was frustrated at the exaggerated sales methods providers were using. Establishing himself as a 'policeman for the industry' the advisory service WhichPLM was formed. In the first year the site recorded 3,000 visitors; this quickly escalated to 3,000 visitors per week. Clients were provided with assistance to ensure they were paired with the most suitable PLM system that aligned with their business values and requirements. Key considerations for achieving the perfect match included determining the reasons behind the need for PLM, identifying specific purposes and benefits, and evaluating the expected return on investment. Mark quickly established that achieving an optimal fit extended far beyond mere technological capabilities. A fundamental necessity was to align the PLM systems with the cultural values of the organization.

Q: Can you explain what PLM is and why it is important for a fashion business success?
Most people will view PLM as a software package, a system employed to improve the functionality of the supply chain. This is a narrow viewpoint; first and foremost, PLM

is a methodology that aims to enhance efficiency, minimize time to market, and ensure product quality and compliance. By providing a centralized platform for managing product data and workflow methods, the software will facilitate effective communication and collaboration among departments and stakeholders, irrespective of their global location. PLM systems typically include features for managing all fashion product data, trend concepts, design, development, costing, sourcing, and delivery. One of the key benefits of PLM systems is the ability to streamline the product development process, resulting in shorter time to market and increased efficiency. By offering a single source of truth for product data, PLM systems reduce the risk of errors and inconsistencies that may arise when different departments work with different versions of the same information. Today, the development of PLM systems is in a constant state of evolution, incorporating innovative technologies like artificial intelligence, machine learning, the internet of things (IoT), and the integration of 3D and digital product creation (DPC). However, the management of product data constantly remains at the heart of the PLM system.

Q: As a PLM specialist, how do you help facilitate relationships between WhichPLM and the fashion sector?

The service at WhichPLM facilitates the building of relationships between fashion clients and PLM providers, building integrity and trust. Breaking the norm in the profit-focused world of fashion, we provide this service free of charge to educate an industry and collaborate with PLM vendors. Working with retailers and brands, WhichPLM aims to identify the unique needs of the retailer or brand and support a mapping process against PLM vendors to build an interface that will link current systems, cultures, and relationships within the global fashion industry.

Q: What are the core problems that fashion companies need to resolve by using a PLM system?

Fashion is moving from a traditional supply chain model to a true value chain, where value is derived solely from a digital end-to-end process encompassing all tiers (0–6) of the supply chain. To maximize the benefits of PLM systems, it is crucial to establish a seamless connection between upstream and downstream operations. This entails integrating upstream tiers such as garment factories, fabric mills, chemical production, raw materials, and farming to ensure brands sell products responsibly and transparently. By facilitating connectivity and fostering transparency, PLM systems play a pivotal role in enabling this transformation.

Q: There are many different PLM systems designed specifically to help fashion retailers conduct efficient business practices. Do you have any examples of how they help buying teams to maximize productivity while minimizing user errors?

There are many ways that PLM systems can maximize productivity and minimize errors: they provide centralized data management, preventing the need for individual spreadsheets or disparate systems; they allow for collaborative communication and automated workflow. However, a feature that truly maximizes productivity is product visualization, visual tools that allow buying teams to create virtual prototypes, visualize product designs, and make modifications before production. The visual planning tools provide a seamless data link between buyers, vendors, and retailers throughout the supply chain, ensuring clarity and avoiding version control issues. PLM has revolutionized the way buyers interact with visual merchandising and product display. Buyers are utilizing virtual stores to showcase fashion categories and ranges, enabling them to visualize how the products will appear when available for sale. This ensures precise product placement, timing, and alignment. With instant information sharing, efficiency, quality, and time to market are substantially improved.

Q: AI technology is impacting fashion at a drastic rate. What are some of the tools that have been integrated into PLM systems, and what support do they provide?

Fashion is an overcomplicated industry and many in the industry will tell you they spend more time looking for data and information than adding value; most fashion professionals will tell you that they spend 25 per cent of their time looking for information – this time is wasted. AI has the power to automate data. Simple tools will automate product categorization, list country of origin or new sources of supply, predict sales and customize size ranges, anticipate silhouettes, and align prints, shades, and drapes. AI algorithms can analyse historical sales data, market trends, and other relevant factors to generate accurate demand forecasts. AI generated virtual prototyping will enable designers and buyers to create realistic and interactive digital representations of products. AI algorithms can analyse trend and fashion-related data from social media, runway shows, fashion magazines, and e-commerce platforms. AI will be used for size and fit optimization, supply chain optimization, and the personalization of consumer insights and purchase history. The fashion industry will strive forward if supported by machine learning and this technology will improve efficiency and accuracy but will also improve transparency, protect intellectual property, and support sustainable developments.

Q: Are there any challenges that retailers, brands, or buyers face when first using PLM? How do you help them to overcome these challenges and beat the learning curve?
Change ... change is hard, there is a fear and it's a cultural process. The process of change should establish a connection between upstream and downstream management. Graduates frequently serve as catalysts for change, and senior management is eager to initiate these changes. However, it's the intermediate levels that require assistance in fully embracing and integrating the changes. PLM systems can work with this change and provide configurations that will ensure the culture of the business is comfortable with the data and imagery.

Q: Where do you see the future of product lifecycle management heading? Is there anything we can expect that will further streamline the PLM process?
We are arriving at a point in an industry where we need to forget the labels. Fashion is on a new journey to embrace a digital-value-chain – in the future, PLM platforms will allow brands to plug and play multiple applications that will utilize and share the data across the platform ecosystems.

Chapter 4 summary

This chapter has examined in outline the why, how, and who of the planning processes involved with creating a range – in particular, those relative to own-label buying. Getting the right number of lines and ranges to fit varying-sized retail platforms is always a problem, and it is here where the buyer and merchandiser relationship is best explained. The research and evaluation that leads up to the final range and the sampling process has been put into context. This chapter has also looked at the high level of detailed numerical planning, analysis, and control used in modern buying and merchandising practice. Finally, the intense focus on achieving key buying KPIs and ultimately the business's planned profitability has been explained. Remember: despite planning, the buyer's eye and instincts still play a major role in a fashion buyer's critical success!

Questions and discussion points

Now that we have looked at the importance of planning in fashion buying, consider the following questions, assuming that you are the buyer.

1. If you were buying a jeans range for the current season, what essential styles would a boutique local to you have to stock in order to present a viable range? How many styles would be needed? Make a list.

2. Once you have answered this question, work out how many different price points, sizes, colours, and fabric options would be needed based on the number of styles that you have suggested.

3. Complete a Good – Better – Best comparison on the range.

4. With reference to the answers provided in questions 1 and 2 how would the range be different if it is for a multinational brand, department store, or retail outlet?

5. Visit a jeans retailer local to you and make a list of the number of styles that they stock – do you think that the range you came up with is better or worse than theirs?

6. What retail prices would you sell your ideal jeans range at? Do look at the competition to work out a set of realistic prices.

N.B. Feel free to substitute any garment type other than jeans in this exercise.

Exercises

Buyers need to be able to identify the winners and losers of a range and update the items appropriately with the season's trends.

Part 1:

Looking at your wardrobe, identify a range of products that you can showcase as part of a capsule collection. Classify the items into the below categories and explain why. Take the time to name and photo or sketch the range.

Ensure you balance your range between tops and bottoms! Describe your consumer and use your sketches to create an initial range plan.

Part 2:

Compare the products to current trend analysis and decide which product will go forward to the next season with no change and at least one product from each category that requires an update. Describe how you will update your products and sketch out again, detailing the impact on trends and explaining how the changes will develop enhanced sales. You can refer to the range planning matrix (Figure 4.12) to identify the types of updates you may include.

STAPLE	SEMI-STYLED	STYLED	FASHION

Trends in Fashion Buying 5

In the previous chapters, we have explored the function of the fashion buyer and their relationships within retail and own brand organizations. We also examined trend forecasting and research techniques, highlighting the significance of buyers being knowledgeable about their consumer demographics and target audiences. Through exploring supplier communication and merchandise planning, we understand how buyers source, manufacture, and allocate products with merchandisers, resulting in a thriving product range for the retail environment. In this final chapter, we will look at emerging trends in the fashion retail landscape and how they can contribute to a buyer's success. These trends include promotional and consumer connectivity strategies, digital technology, and social responsibility.

Figure 5.1 Paolo Carzana – Runway – LFW February 2023.
Paolo Carzana presents a collection that draws inspiration from elements of romance, nature, and the Renaissance. The designs feature delicate fabrics and innovative combinations of asymmetric layers.

Consumer connection promotional activities

The rise of social media and consumer connectivity has intensified the need for strategic promotional activities. Retailers and brands are focusing on creating personalized experiences for their customers through targeted marketing campaigns, loyalty programmes, and social media engagement, all aimed at boosting seasonal sales and accelerating product turnover while maintaining profit margins. Although some promotions may involve discounted prices, there are other effective promotional techniques that can drive sales without undermining the buying and merchandising team's pricing strategy.

Branding, advertising, and marketing

Advances in technology and shifting consumer preferences have changed the way consumers shop for fashion and, in turn, this has led to a change in the strategies employed in branding, advertising, and marketing. Brand collaboration is extremely popular in the fast fashion market; however, partnerships have evolved. While teaming up with high-end designers remains important and profitable, consumer expectations around equality, diversity, and inclusion have expanded the possibilities for collaborations between mainstream influencers and household names. Influencers are perceived as more relatable and approachable than celebrities; followers feel more connected to them and are more likely to trust their recommendations. Influencers often have a niche following that aligns closely with a specific brand or product, allowing the collaboration to be more targeted and effective.

Data is the driving force for a new level of sophistication in branding, advertising, and marketing strategies. Companies have shifted to be more consumer centric with brands or retailers focusing on creating personalized, engaging experiences that resonate with their target audience. The industry has undergone a transformation due to social media, enabling brands to effectively reach their target audience and generate sales through various social media platforms. Fashion brands, in particular, heavily rely on visually appealing content to create an immersive experience for their customers. Social media platforms such as Instagram, Facebook, TikTok, and YouTube are leading the way, with Pinterest, Snapchat, and Twitter following closely behind. Social media is not limited to brand promotion but has become a place for customers to purchase products through the emerging trend of 'social commerce'.

Working closely with social media is artificial intelligence (AI).

H&M x Mugler

Showcasing alluring body-hugging designs, striking silhouettes, and daringly revealing cut-outs, H&M x Mugler created a tremendous buzz, surpassing even the success of the Simone Rocha collaboration.

BRANDING, ADVERTISING, AND MARKETING   149

Maison Margiela x Reebok

The collaboration between Maison Margiela and Reebok presents a collection of Reebok's iconic designs reimagined with the artistic vision of creative director John Galliano and the distinct aesthetic codes of Maison Margiela.

Figure 5.2 Notable collaborations Margiela x Reebok.

Model Sora Choi wears neon yellow painted hair, cheetah fur jacket, black dress, and Maison Margiela x Reebok Instapump sneakers after the Dries van Noten show during Paris Fashion Week Fall/Winter 2020 on 26 February 2020 in Paris, France.

Balmain x Barbie.

In anticipation for the forthcoming movie, Balmain partners with Barbie for a special, limited-edition collection.

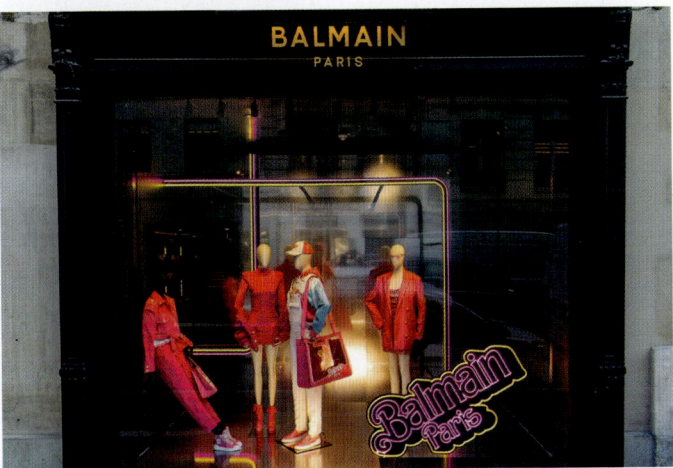

Figure 5.3 A view of the Balmain store window shop where the Balmain x Barbie capsule collection is displayed at the Balmain Saint Honoré Boutique on 14 January 2022 in Paris, France.

Social media and the AI influencer

Artificial intelligence (AI) is reaching new heights in fashion and the introduction of the AI influencer has revolutionized how fashion is promoted. Unlike their human counterparts, AI influencers allow for 24/7 availability and the capability to create highly curated content, but there are still limitations in the areas of authenticity and relatability and concerns around the use of AI to create fake content or manipulate public opinion.

When it comes to advertising and marketing, historically retailers were known to pay hefty sums of money to have ads run on billboards, in magazines, or via television or live streaming. While this is a great way for the brand to get exposure, it can put a heavy burden on the buyer who needs to be aware of running (present and future) campaigns that may cause a shift in the popularity of a product.

Advertising and marketing, if successful, will create a need for a product and, if buyers have not purchased enough of that product to be able to provide it to consumers, then consumers may turn elsewhere, sending sales to competing retailers. It is crucial that buyers can respond quickly with repeat orders if necessary. However, the buyer may also employ a FOMO (fear of missing out) strategy, creating a sense of urgency for shoppers to buy a particular item

Figure 5.4 Most sought-after retail promotion.
While many consumers resonate with (and are drawn to) various marketing campaigns presented by their favourite retailers, it is the 'sale' sign that often prompts consumers to visit retailers in the hope of finding a bargain.

before it sells out or is no longer available, purposefully allowing the product to run out to encourage consumers to constantly check the 'new in' sections on online apps and websites.

While advertising and marketing campaigns will often promote new goods for the season, one of the greatest marketing campaigns is created when a retailer goes into markdown mode, typically adding clearly marked red-type signage and discount banners on web-based platforms. While each retailer or brand treats sales promotions differently, the ultimate goal for each is to move through units quickly, making room for new goods to arrive. Buyers work with merchandisers on pricing strategies for both sales and promotions and then with the marketing teams to create the appropriate signage.

Marketing and Advertising Initiatives

Retailers and fashion brands use various methods and media to deliver information to consumers. Understanding consumer purchasing behaviour (discussed in Chapter 2) allows buyers to work with marketing and/or advertising teams to:

- increase brand awareness and new branding initiatives
- differentiate themselves from their competitors
- increase footfall in store or online
- enhance consumer engagement and brand loyalty
- attract new consumers and followers
- drive sales
- increase units per transaction (UPT), or the amount of goods that a consumer buys per sales transaction.

Miquela Sousa @lilmiquel, first AI influencer to go viral on Instagram.

Figure 5.5 Global marketing impacts.
Jeans are not only an iconic product, when made well they can last a lifetime; however, they are also known to be one of the largest consumers of water in their production; starting with the cultivation of cotton to the manufacturing, water is an essential component. At the forefront of denim sustainability Levi's have launched their 'Buy Better, Wear Longer' campaign which aims to create quality clothing that lasts for generations. Whilst still producing product, they are shifting the responsibility to the consumer.

Visual merchandising

In Chapter 4, we discussed the ways in which the merchandiser's role differs from that of the visual merchandiser. However, it is important to be aware that visual merchandising teams still work very closely with buying/merchandising teams to create aesthetically pleasing visual presentations with the intention of promoting the brand, educating the consumer, and of course, driving sales. The buyer will work with visual merchandising teams, both at a corporate and store level, to put priority on certain products with high budget investment. Maintaining constant communication allows visual merchandising teams to understand seasonal investments that are purchased to make the largest profit and allows rapid consumer feedback. Although buyers do not art direct the visual merchandising approach of a retailer or brand, they will work with visual teams to discuss product placement in specific zones, to make deep seasonal buys a focus for all consumers.

VISUAL MERCHANDISING

Driving sales through digital visual merchandising

Outform TM is pioneering an advanced digital mannequin platform for retailers. The technology will enhance visual merchandising and engage customers through immersive experiences. Using augmented reality (AR) and artificial intelligence (AI), it delivers interactive displays, personalized recommendations, and styling guides. The platform can also provide data for optimizing purchasing strategies, improving products, and increasing loyalty.

Scan the QR code to see Outform TM.

A strong visual merchandising strategy will grow sales; the buyer must ensure that the visual teams understand range characteristics and drive sales for products with high profits. The growth of online consumption has influenced consumer preferences and the way people shop; consumers are expecting personalized shopping experiences in store as well as online, enabling brands to connect with their customers on a deeper level, increasing customer loyalty, and driving sales. Personalization and an increased focus on digital displays is impacting the instore experience. Digital displays that interact with mobile devices have led to an increase in the use of high-quality images and videos, as well as interactive features such as virtual try-on tools and digital mannequins.

Figure 5.6 Adidas stores globally are known for innovation and bold visuals. Adidas Uniforia match ball at the Adidas flagship store, Beijing, China.

Showtelling and pop-up

'Showtelling' is a marketing strategy where brands create physical spaces that showcase fashion ranges but do not allow consumers to buy on-site. The aim is to provide consumers with an immersive experience, allowing consumers to interact with the brand's products and understand the brand's story and values. The showtelling spaces are small in square footage and often carry a single-size run of goods. Customers enter the space, see, and feel the product, have the ability to try it on, and then order it online. The products are shipped directly to the customer or for collection at the showtelling space. This keeps overhead costs down, allowing the brand or retailer to focus on interacting with the customer. Typically, luxury brands are among the first to adopt innovative marketing strategies, such as showtelling, with successful installations by Burberry and Louis Vuitton. Sportswear giants Adidas and Nike, and denim leaders Levi's have also followed suit with similar approaches.

On the other side of showtelling is the pop-up store. These are typically held at temporary venues, ranging anywhere from a weekend to a three-month period (or longer). Pop-up shops can provide fashion retailers, brands, and emerging designers with a low-cost, low-risk way to increase brand awareness, test new markets and products, and create unique and memorable customer experiences. Areas of regeneration are capitalizing on the retail opportunities associated with the pop-up to increase footfall. BOXPARK, which has venues in Croydon, Wembley, and Shoreditch, is known as the world's first pop-up mall. BOXPARK is a mix of fashion, lifestyle, and dining, attracting the affluent independent consumer (Figure 5.7).

Scan the QR code to see BOXPARK webpage.

BOXPARK

Similar pop-up venues are The Street, located in Chestnut Hill, Massachusetts; The Market Line, located in the Lower East Side of Manhattan; and The Bloc, located in downtown Los Angeles.

Working with the fashion press

Due to the rise of social media and e-commerce, the relationship between the press and fashion retail has evolved significantly. Fashion businesses endeavour to display their new ranges to the relevant press and media to get as much publicity as possible. However, the methods of storytelling have evolved due to social media. Traditional media including print magazines and television are still important, but their influence has decreased, and many retailers and brands employ their own content creation teams and digital magazines or lookbooks, which they use to showcase their products. Fashion buyers often become involved with advising on ranges or products that are to be used at press shows and in publicity packs and tasked

Figure 5.7 BOXPARK London.

with providing samples ahead of the product launch. Buyers will use data to ensure they select the correct press and media that are tailored to individual consumers' preferences. The fashion industry is under increased scrutiny for its environmental impact and fashion journalists from all walks of media are looking out for new and exciting products and stories that focus on sustainability and ethical fashion for their next fashion features, magazines, and supplements.

Press packs are a valuable tool for retailers and brands to communicate information about their brand, products, and collections and will often provide key information on the product launch and locations as well as sizes, constructions, colours, and pricing. To increase speed and promote sustainability, many retailers have switched to digital press packs, which can be accessed online and include multimedia resources such as videos and interactive product catalogues.

Fashion companies used to hire prestigious venues to host open house days where new ranges were shown, and the fashion media were invited to attend. In recent years brands have shifted to holding virtual open house days that include virtual tours of collections, immersive interviews with designers, and interactive product demos, which can be accessed remotely by members of the press all over the world.

Most fashion companies will utilize a variety of online PR service agencies, which can also provide a wide range of PR-related services, such as online press releases, photographs, and archives. With so many influential fashion bloggers watching the fashion blogosphere, a strong online PR presence is now a vital element of good fashion marketing communication.

Buyers and assistant buyers will attend press days and meet with important fashion media contacts to give them a more personalized tour of the ranges. With so much fashion PR activity taking place today, there is always a huge amount of competition to get important fashion media along to more minor press days or press launches. Buyers with new and exciting ranges, brands, or ideas therefore always attract the more important fashion media.

Providing samples for the press and influencers

The fashion press requires new season samples well in advance in order to develop topical newsworthy stories. Controlling press samples effectively is extremely important, with many being sent away on location and damaged by make-up and general wear and tear.

Good photographic publicity is the lifeblood of successful fashion businesses; buying teams with the ability to respond quickly and efficiently to the insatiable and sometimes unreasonable demands of the fashion press get the greatest return. Just as important as the press are the fashion influencers, and providing samples to the right influencer who will share images through their social media is not only cost-effective, it will increase brand exposure and authenticity, build trust, and provide valuable consumer feedback. It is important for brands to carefully research and select influencers that align with their values, target audience, and marketing goals – partnering with the wrong influencer can harm a brand's reputation and waste marketing resources.

Fashion technology and the digital fashion landscape

As with many industries, the development of technology has revolutionized the fashion landscape. Technological advances have allowed buyers to be quicker, more efficient, and achieve greater accuracy. It allows us to communicate, travel, and access information more easily, which has facilitated globalization and transformed the way we do business in so many ways. Buyers are tapping into technology to overcome communication obstacles and lengthy lead times in pursuit of quicker replenishment turnaround, a stronger consumer understanding, and, of course, greater ease in carrying out the duties associated with their job.

Today, technology is delivered in so many formats that it is important for brands and retailers to adapt to changing market trends and, specifically, to understand how their consumers have changed the way they engage with retail.

Technology and improved business practice

The internet and the concept of 'the internet of things' (IoT) enabled a vast network of connected devices to collect and exchange data, to be used to improve efficiency, optimize performance, and expand the reach and capabilities of fashion buyers. The adoption of new and emerging technology has improved and simplified core tasks such as staying on top of trends, discovering new brands, and making more informed decisions; buyers are able to:

- View, order, and communicate with international manufacturers and suppliers much more efficiently.
- Through supplier portals, share product data, discuss trends, re-order, and collaborate in real time regardless of their location.
- Research trends via social media sites, trend forecasting agencies, and/or online blogs and magazines.
- Get real-time product sell-through via systems that connect buying offices to retail allowing them to quickly reorder product.
- Access a wealth of data and analytics that support purchasing decisions, utilizing tools like Google Analytics to track website traffic and consumer behaviour, to optimize their product offering and communication strategies.

Technology that is changing the fashion landscape

Body scanning uses 3D imaging to capture the measurements, shape, and contours of the body. Fashion is using this tech for personalization, custom tailoring, fit optimization, and virtual try-on. Returns are a real issue in fashion, not just for business resources and cost but for the environment. Analysis of consumer data through body scanning technology permits fashion designers and manufacturers to identify patterns and trends in body measurements, allowing them to adjust sizing and fit to suit their customers. The commercialization of body scanning is leading to enhanced virtual try-on applications, where customers can try on clothing virtually, supporting consumers to make purchasing decisions more confidently and reducing the need for returns.

Magic mirrors use AR technology to provide an interactive and personalized shopping experience. The mirror uses cameras and sensors to capture the customer's image and overlay virtual images of fashion products or accessories onto the customer's reflection in real time. Some may also offer personalized recommendations based on the customer's body type, size, and style preferences and can also provide information such as the material, price, and availability.

AR/VR/Oculus – augmented reality (AR) and virtual reality (VR): AR and VR technologies have been used by fashion brands to provide consumers with immersive shopping experiences. We can virtually try on clothes and accessories, share pictures, and get online feedback before committing to a purchase.

Sustainable and eco-friendly technology – there is an increased focus on sustainable and eco-friendly technologies. Buyers are working with brands that use sustainable materials and production methods, and many brands have responded by adopting eco-friendly technologies like recycled fabrics and 3D printing and 3D prototyping to reduce the need for sampling and waste in the industry.

3D prototyping uses three-dimensional modelling software and printing technology to create physical representations of designs before they are produced. It can be used for a range of purposes, including creating mock-ups of garments, testing the fit and functionality of designs, and exploring new materials and textures. 3D will allow designers and buyers to save time and money by reducing the need for physical samples, improving the accuracy of their designs, and reducing waste in the production process. Leading the 3D revolution is Clo Virtual Fashion Inc., a software company that specializes in creating 3D garment visualization and simulation software for the fashion industry. We will discuss Clo3D in more detail at the end of this chapter.

Blockchain technology is being adopted to improve the transparency and traceability of fashion products. Using sensors and RFID tags, buyers and consumers can track the entire supply chain of a product, from raw materials to finished products, providing authenticity and supporting sustainability in fashion.

Eye-tracking technology is being used to improve marketing, website design, and user experience to enhance sales. The tech uses specialized software and hardware to track a user's eye movements as they navigate a website or view a product. The tech can identify whether elements of a page are causing frustration or confusion and can also be used to improve product placement. By tracking which products users are looking at and for how long, retailers can identify which items are most popular and adjust their OTB accordingly.

Mobile commerce, smartphones, and web data codes

With the rise of smartphones and mobile devices, mobile commerce is at the forefront of fashion business.

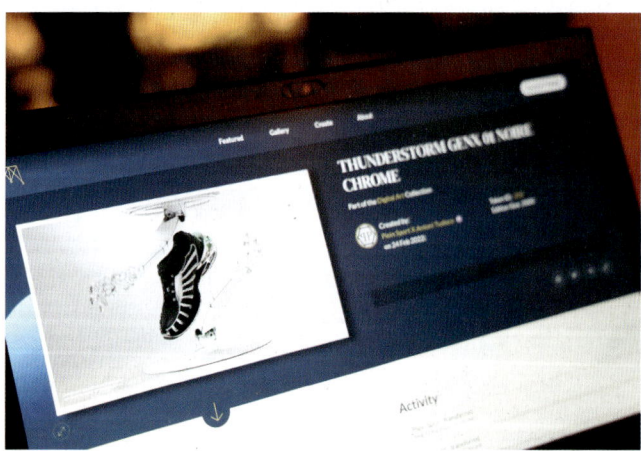

Figure 5.8 Digital business.
Buyers address production or design issues the very minute that they occur. The speed at which buyers, designers, and merchandisers can now conduct business has revolutionized the fashion industry, making it a smaller and much more competitive place.

Consumers can access their favourite retailers and brands with a touch of an application, linking them directly to online stores with payment plans such as Klarna and next-day delivery schemes for subscribers. Retailers are making it easier to engage in their web platforms by using QR codes, data matrix codes, Microsoft tags, Snapcodes, and BeeTags.

The most common code for fashion is the QR code. They are often used to provide customers with product information such as sizing, care instructions, product reviews, and promotional offers. QR codes can also be used for inventory management, product tracking, and supply chain management support. Although not as common as the QR code, Data Matrix codes and Aztec codes are also used in the fashion industry for similar objectives. Data Matrix codes can be used on clothing labels to store information about the product's fabric content, country of origin, and other important details. Similarly, Aztec codes can be used on shipping labels to track and manage inventory as it moves through the supply chain.

Figure 5.9 Roberto Verino – Mercedes Benz Fashion Week Madrid, April 2021. QR code to view the collection.

Figures 5.10 QR code as fashion statement.

Retailers are increasingly leveraging technology to enhance their brand awareness and sales. They are using a range of digital tools, including the internet, smartphones, and QR codes (see Figures 5.9 and 5.10), to promote and advertise their products. Additionally, buying teams are using technology to track sales within stores and quickly replenish stock, as well as to analyse the profitability of seasonal buying ranges and identify slow-selling items. Furthermore, technology is empowering buying and merchandising teams to better understand their consumer demographics and preferences, enabling them to make data-driven decisions that improve their overall business performance.

Corporate social responsibility (CSR)

Buying teams have a responsibility to themselves, to the company that they work for, and, most importantly, to the customer. Corporate social responsibility is the self-imposed regulatory system that a fashion business will build into their strategic plan and

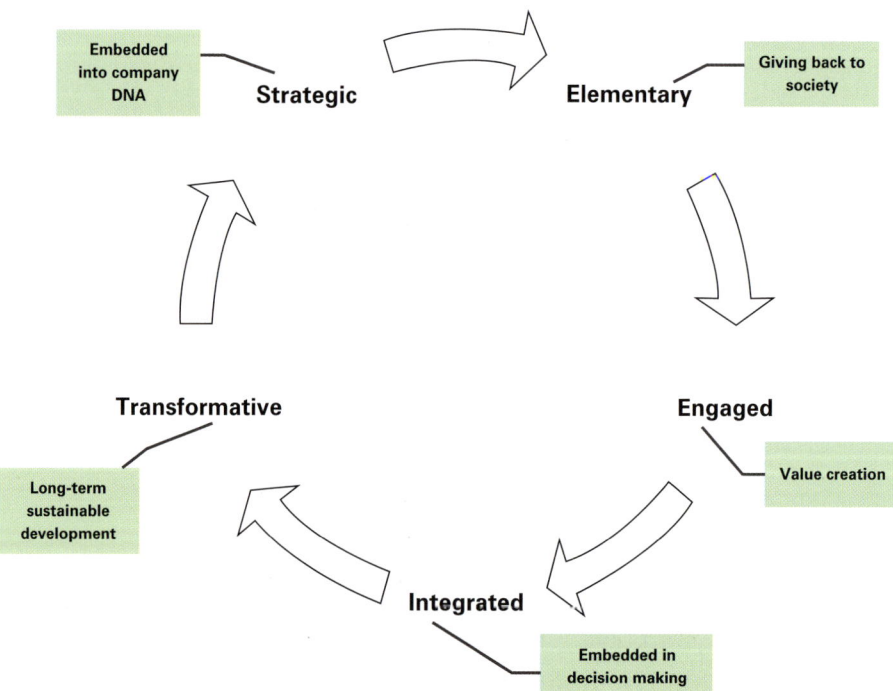

Figure 5.11 CSR cycle.
Corporate social responsibility initiatives involve multiple entities within the context of social, environmental, and economic values. The company commitment often focuses on five stages, and it is important to understand how each is dependent on the other and how lack of initiative for one could seriously affect the others, both positively and negatively.

company mission. The objective is to seamlessly integrate people, planet, and profit into a module that can work to create sustainable measures for all three elements. The fashion industry is notorious for its negative impact on the environment and has a history of worker exploitation in developing countries. As a result, CSR practices have become standard for addressing concerns and the creation of more sustainable and ethical businesses.

For a business to implement CSR initiatives, it will typically map out an overall plan for long-term growth and will start with small tasks that won't drastically deplete revenue, allowing it to grow in a positive direction. Each employee, knowing that the company has identified specific initiatives, will then be required to help achieve these goals, both in the short and long term (examples shown in Figure 5.11). In addition to the company initiatives, each employee bears the responsibility of monitoring their own ethical behaviour to help to reach the intended goal.

CSR Stakeholders

Many individuals, companies, and communities are part of CSR outreaches:

- Employees – those working in the field and at corporate offices, from senior management to maintenance.
- Customers – past, present, and future customers who buy into the company brand.
- Communities – the areas and individuals who are part of the physical environment where shops or home offices are located.
- Suppliers – both national and international, as well as the employees of the suppliers.
- Investors – those who want to see the company grow but typically only provide monetary means or consulting services.

Each stakeholder within the fashion organization has a responsibility to uphold the CSR initiatives set out by the company strategy. Buyers and their wider team will deal with suppliers every day; they should be aware of their CSR initiatives, just as they are of their own. When forming new relationships, they should investigate how the supplier conducts business and how it treats both its employees and the environment, avoiding suppliers that do not pay fair wages and that do not provide adequate facilities or breaks for their employees. Buyers should be seeking out supplier partnerships that provide training and education programmes for workers to improve their skills and empower them to advocate for their rights. Buying teams should have robust supplier vetting processes in place. Initiating this right at the start of a new relationship, the buyer will be fully aware of a company's practices and make decisions to initiate business or not. Maintaining supplier appraisal techniques will ensure that circumstances have not changed, enabling the buyer to uphold their CSR initiatives. Moving forward, buying teams should work with suppliers on developing CSR initiatives that contribute to a better fashion industry. Examples include the implementation of sustainable production methods, or using eco-friendly materials, reducing waste and emissions, and ensuring that products are made in ethical working conditions. Some fashion businesses are investing in renewable energy sources and projects that reduce their carbon footprint, such as carbon offsetting.

Engaging in philanthropic activities such as donating to charities or partnering with organizations that promote social and environmental causes is also part of a CSR strategy, initiating steps to improve transparency and accountability by publicly reporting on their CSR efforts and progress.

Shoe retailer TOMS is a B Certified corporation and a member of the Fair Labor Association (FLA). Their commitment to 'purpose, planet, people' ensures that their products and processes reflect their commitment to bettering the workers' rights in their manufacturing and production plants. TOMS also donates one-third of their profits to 'Grassroots Good'; through the development of partnerships with

Figures 5.12–5.13 Wear TOMS wear good – TOMS and CSR.

non-profits they are working to create impact in the areas of mental health, access to opportunity, and ending gun violence, in the United States.

CSR vs ESG

As with fashion, corporate terminology changes over time and recently companies have been flipping their CSR strategies for environmental, social, and governance (ESG) strategies. ESG and CSR are related but distinct concepts. In ESG the 'E' stands for environmental factors, such as impact on climate change, natural resource use, and waste management. The 'S' stands for social factors, such as impact on employees, customers, and communities. The 'G' stands for governance factors, policies, practices, and structures related to ethics, transparency, and accountability. ESG typically applies to the three broad areas of concern that investors and other stakeholders consider when evaluating the sustainability and ethical impact of a business or company; while CSR refers to a company's voluntary actions to improve its impact on society and the environment beyond what is required by law.

A certified B corporation with a global organic textile standard (GOTS), VEJA is known for eco-friendly materials, recycled packaging, and collaborating with gold certified tanneries. Their strategies reduce their climate impact by limiting chemicals, water, and wastewater in production.

Figure 5.14 VEJA – Looking way past the product and using transparency to show how sneakers are made – VEJA and ESG.

Fashion circularity

The fashion industry is one of the most polluting industries globally, contributing significantly to carbon emissions, waste production, and water pollution; this in part is due to the linear approach within the supply chain. Raw materials are obtained, garments are produced, distributed, sold, worn, and finally disposed of as waste making.

Fashion circularity leaves behind the linear model, adopting a sustainable and circular approach. The theory of circular fashion is to keep materials and products in use for as long as possible through a process of recycling, repairing, and repurposing. For circularity to be real, fashion products must be designed to be durable, adaptable, and recyclable, ensuring that they can be used for a more extended period or be incorporated into a closed-loop recycling process. Closed-loop recycling permits the continuous recycling of materials; this reduces the need for virgin resources and minimizes waste. The process involves gathering used textiles and fibres, then converting them back into new products, so that fashion items are no longer considered as disposable commodities. Circularity is not just about the products; as well as waste reduction, its aim is to promote responsible consumption and foster innovation in the fashion industry. A key concept is the circular supply chain, incorporating sustainable practice into each stage from sourcing raw materials to the end-of-life. Therefore, companies who wish to work within the circular model must consider their operational factors and the environmental and social impact. The fashion business can reduce their environmental footprint, promote ethical and sustainable practices, and create a positive impact on society and the environment by embracing a circular supply chain approach.

It will not be easy for the fashion industry to become a circular economy as there are significant changes required in the way fashion is produced and consumed. There will need to be a substantial shift made by the consumer and their fashion consumption, and a change in the fashion industry's business model, by the adoption of new technologies and practices. The momentum is real and growing awareness by society towards circular fashion is shifting the landscape.

Shifting the sands in circularity

Leading outdoor clothing brand **Patagonia** has been a forerunner in sustainable fashion for decades, adopting circular fashion practices such as a free repair, recycled materials, and designing their clothes to be durable and long-lasting. **Levi's** launched 'Levi's SecondHand', allowing customers to buy and sell pre-owned Levi's clothing. **H&M** has recently launched many initiatives that promote circular fashion; they offer repairs and alterations through their 'Take Care' initiative and their ambition is to achieve net-zero greenhouse gas emissions by 2040. **Girlfriend Collective** have incorporated their 'Recycle, Reuse, ReGirlfriend' strategy that collects old Girlfriend Collective compressive leggings and upcycles them into new products to be worn again and again … and again.

Intellectual property rights (IPR)

It is important to protect design originality and the authenticity of the lines that are built into a range. Due to the fast-changing nature of fashion, IPR is a minefield, with designers and brands frequently being copied by other individuals or organizations that hope to capitalize on trending designs.

The IPR attached to the copied product, whoever owns it, is effectively stolen to make profit for another organization and/or individual. In many cultures, copying is not seen as a crime, although increasingly individuals and organizations are developing techniques, laws, and/or systems to protect their IP from the unscrupulous.

Anti-Copying in Design (ACID), a useful organization with good advisory resources that was founded in 1996, is now helping fashion businesses and designers to avoid IP issues (www.acid.uk.com). Unique fashion and textile surface designs can be registered in the UK, Europe, and many other non-EU countries. However, the registration processes and costs vary dramatically and for many smaller companies and designers doing so is simply not financially viable.

Design registration is an immensely complex process, but fashion buyers and readers can find many online advisory resources. One of the best sources of UK and European IP advice is to be found at the Centre for Fashion Enterprise, based in the University of the Arts London (www.arts.ac.uk/colleges/london-college-of-fashion/business-and-innovation/centre-for-fashion-enterprise). On a more international basis, The World Intellectual Property Organization, based in Geneva, is also a good source for pan-international IP advice relating to fashion (www.wipo.int).

When fashion buyers raise official business contracts, these generally include caveats warning suppliers about the need for authenticity and uniqueness in their products and designs; this helps to protect the buyer and their organization from any future legal challenges. In reality, all fashion garments and products probably take inspiration from each other: after all, is anything totally unique?

Buyers need to remain aware of these situations and strive to keep the market clean of stolen designs and inauthentic merchandise. While this may be part of the organization's overall CSR direction, buyers will typically follow their own instincts on this front, knowing how detrimental it can be for the company to engage in unethical practices; and more importantly, in order to maintain their own clear conscience.

CASE STUDY
CLO Virtual Fashion Incorporated: Simon J.H. Kim – Global CEO

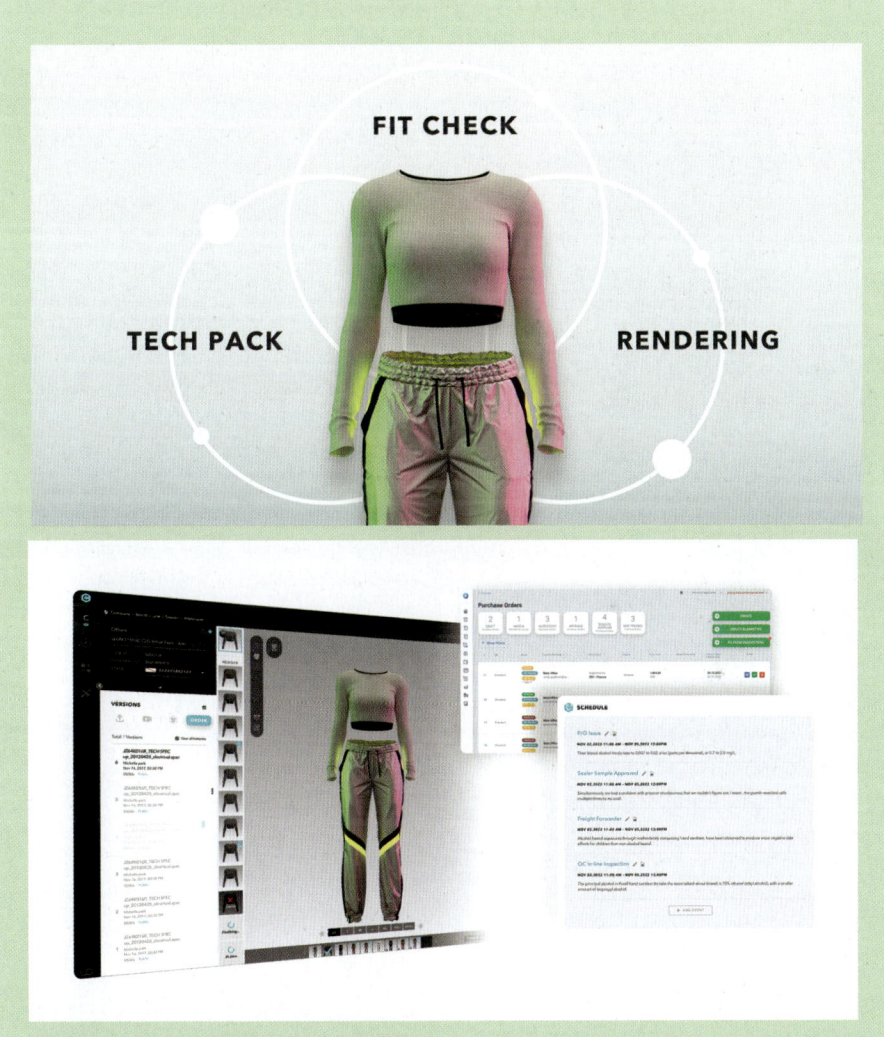

Figures 5.15–5.16 CLO Virtual Fashion Incorporated.
Established in 2009, CLO Virtual Fashion Incorporated is a renowned software company that focuses on 3D garment simulation and visualization. They excel in offering virtual tools for garment design, prototyping, and presentation, making them a leader in the industry.

Figure 5.17 Simon J.H. Kim.

Simon J.H. Kim is the global CEO of CLO Virtual Fashion, the company responsible for developing CLO and Marvelous Designer, the leading 3D fashion design software for apparel, gaming, and entertainment companies. Investor turned entrepreneur, Simon has always been actively involved in technological innovation throughout his career. Prior to joining CLO Virtual Fashion, Simon held roles as a venture capitalist at IDG Ventures Group and a strategic investor at NC Soft. Simon earned both his master's and bachelor's degrees from the London School of Economics.

Victoria Wang, brand communications manager at CLO Virtual Fashion, provided the answers to the following:

What is CLO?

CLO is a 3D fashion design software that enables fashion designers, brands, and manufacturers to create digital fashion designs. These true-to-life designs have many applications, such as hyperrealistic garment visualization, virtual fit and functionality testing, marketing and e-commerce material, and physical garment design development and production.

How is CLO different/unique?

CLO always strives to make the software faster, easier, more accurate, and limitless so that users can unleash their creativity to the fullest. CLO's user-friendly interface facilitates a gentler learning curve and is the fastest 3D fashion design software available – not only in the speed of cloth simulation but also the ability for designers to work in both 2D and 3D windows simultaneously, allowing for real-time design changes, which are essential to any fast-paced design development process.

The detail and accuracy of the software allow each and every design feature, from comprehensive patternmaking tools to applying design details such as pleats, pintucks, folds, and steam (ironing) effects, to work in tandem. The 3D design software also works seamlessly with other products in CLO Virtual Fashion's ecosystem (including CLO-SET, a digital content management and collaborative workspace, and CONNECT, an open marketplace and community platform) to provide users with a more creative, efficient, and enhanced experience, while maximizing the full value of each garment. Last but not least, CLO has a business model that empowers individual designers/ateliers and enterprise clients, leading to a powerful extended user community that collaborates and helps each other for the good of the industry.

How many clients does CLO have?
CLO is used by over 1 million users (individual designers, fashion brands, and schools) in 100+ countries, including companies such as Hugo Boss, Adidas, Mango, Theory, Emilio Pucci, Salomon, Levi's, LL Bean, and many more, as well as schools like FIT, Parsons, and Cornell.

What are the markets for CLO and how does the buyer benefit?
CLO can be used by anyone along the garment design and production pipeline – from fashion designers to manufacturers to marketers. As mentioned above, the software can be leveraged as a digital twin to a physical sample for virtual fit sessions, online merchandising assortments, internal sales reviews, digital photoshoots, marketing campaigns, and much more – all while collecting data points and metadata to generate analytics and tech packs. CLO can be used by an entire organization to help everyone collaborate more effectively and speak the same (3D) language.

Can you explain the benefits of CLO when it comes to design, accuracy, garment fit, and resource utilization?
With more than twenty years of research and development in accurate garment simulation, CLO is known for its realistic simulations of fabrics, draping, and garment movement, which can aid fashion designers and brands in reducing the time and cost associated with traditional sample-making processes. With CLO, designers can create and customize virtual garments with ease, which can accelerate the product development process and improve the overall quality of their designs.

Digital technologies and sustainability go hand in hand; what has been the biggest impact of adopting CLO to sustainable practice and zero waste?
3D garment simulation technology has evolved to a point where the methods of traditional design can all be emulated in 3D. It means that 3D can be used in the full cycle of the design development process, from fabrics to fit checks, making important design decisions throughout the process. By designing in 3D and reviewing true-to-life digital garments with suppliers via collaborative platforms such as

CLO-SET (www.clo-set.com), all stakeholders in the design development process can now communicate and collaborate earlier in the process and more accurately. With 3D, brands can now make design decisions earlier in the process – within hours or days rather than the traditional weeks and months of back-and-forth communication with physical samples. This changes everything; CLO brings faster lead times, raises communication efficiency, and ultimately results in higher quality designs, all while achieving sustainability goals and not contributing to more waste or putting pressure on suppliers.

How easy is it to convert design practice to use CLO instead of hand drawing?

CLO offers an incredible advantage to designers by enabling them to quickly visualize their designs. By using the garments available in the library, designers can choose a base to start from and make visual alterations directly in the 3D window. Additionally, designers can import files from other 2D CAD software, including graded sizes. It's also possible to import images of your pattern or sketch and trace them in the 2D window in CLO. Furthermore, the software allows designers to import measurements into the Parametric Pattern Editor to create a pattern or draft pattern shapes directly in the 2D window using the built-in drafting tools.

How easy is it to fill the asset bank and what support does CLO offer?

The CLO library is full of resources, featuring a wide range of digital fabrics, avatars, and various hardware and trims such as topstitching and bows. Designers have the freedom to personalize these assets and create their own personal library. In addition, the CONNECT marketplace offers a vast collection of assets, including numerous free fabrics and contributions from various companies producing zippers, buttons, and a myriad of topstitching and trims.

CLO offers a wide range of support including training, file-specific support, tech support, and implementation advice. CLO also offers custom training and implementation guidance for enterprise and academic clients.

What's next for CLO?

CLO's 3D design technology empowers every step of the garment journey, from concept to design, manufacturing to marketing, and fitting to styling. We're excited about what's next because there are countless areas where CLO can pave the way to a better retail future. We believe that 3D design technology is a key component to reaching a sustainable, waste-free fashion future where digital assets replace physical samples, 3D-based collaboration improves communication between designers and manufacturers, and exciting consumer innovations are the norm – such as 'responsive design' where consumers can purchase designs before they're even produced and 3D virtual try-ons which can minimize returns and exchanges.

As CLO also powers the digital entertainment industry (animation, film, gaming), we're seeing a convergence of digital entertainment and fashion through our technology. Brands are extending their presence into digital spaces, and this trend will only continue with the metaverse. Ultimately, we envision a future where every physical garment is connected to a virtual outfit and vice versa.

CLO has launched several initiatives to push the industry forward along all of these avenues, including virtual try-on services and showrooms, our Metaverse Converting Service, and a Web3-powered digital fashion marketplace. We are confident that our technology will power the future of everything related to garments, and we're excited to build it together with our user community.

Chapter 5 summary

In this final chapter we have considered new and emerging trends that influence fashion buying practice, discussed the dynamic world of fashion promotion by examining the role of consumers in fashion promotion and how their behaviours and preferences influence the marketing strategies employed by fashion brands. We have explored various promotion techniques utilized by brands, and delved into the evolving methods of fashion collaboration, social media, and social commerce. We have discussed the power of partnerships between fashion brands and influencers, celebrities, and other industry players, and how these collaborations enable brands to reach wider audiences and create unique and engaging content. Additionally, we have explored the rise of AI influencers, virtual personalities created using artificial intelligence, and their impact on fashion sales.

We have paid attention to fashion retail developments, and explored the growing popularity of pop-up stores, which provide brands with temporary physical spaces to engage directly with consumers and create immersive brand experiences. We have also discussed the integration of technology in fashion retail, such as virtual reality, augmented reality, and interactive displays, which enhance the shopping experience and drive customer engagement.

Lastly, we have addressed the increasing significance of corporate social responsibility (CSR), environmental, social, and governance (ESG) practices, and circularity in fashion. We have explored how brands are incorporating sustainable practices throughout the supply chain, embracing ethical manufacturing processes, and adopting circular business models to minimize waste and reduce their environmental footprint.

Questions and discussion points

Exercise: Fashion traceability using Blockchain. A simulation to show how blockchain technology is used for traceability in the fashion industry.

Background: Discuss the reasons why fashion supply chains should be more transparent and the reasons why they may not be; ask students to identify brands that are more transparent than others. Following this, discuss the concept of blockchain in fashion by explaining how it is being used in the fashion industry to enhance supply chain traceability and authenticity. Emphasize that blockchain can help track and verify the journey of products from raw materials to finished garments, ensuring transparency and reducing counterfeiting. Align this with the six tiers of the fashion supply chain from Chapter 4.

Select a fashion product: Choose a specific fashion product, such as a t-shirt, pair of jeans, or an accessory such as a bag or shoe for the exercise. Explain that the goal is to trace the product's journey using a blockchain system.

Blockchain design: Divide the students into groups of 3–4 and instruct each group to design a blockchain system to track the chosen fashion product, considering the following elements:

Identify the key stakeholders: In relation to the six tiers of the supply chain discussed in Chapter 4, each group should identify the key stakeholders involved in the fashion supply chain; for example manufacturers, suppliers, distributors, and even farmers.

Determine the information: The groups need to decide on the specific details they should capture for each step of the product's journey. Discuss that this may start with the seed for farming if it a natural fibre or the chemicals if it is man-made. The journey may not end at retail, but this may form the end point.

Define the blockchain structure: The groups need to decide how they will structure the blockchain. They may choose a private blockchain (limited to trusted participants) or a public blockchain (open to anyone). They should also consider the consensus mechanism, such as proof-of-work or proof-of-stake.

Present blockchain design: Each group needs to prepare to present their blockchain design to their peers. They should draw attention to their reasoning behind the chosen stakeholders, recorded information, and blockchain structure. Encourage other groups to ask questions and provide feedback.

Trace and record the fashion product: Ask each group to create a sequential order to represent the blockchain and an expected timeline of the fashion product's journey, representing each step, and ask them to highlight the traceability process using the designed blockchain system.

Discuss and reflect on the benefits: Once all groups have shared their information, begin a conversation on the benefits of using blockchain for traceability in the fashion industry and encourage reflection on transparency, counterfeiting, and the promotion of ethical and sustainable practices.

Summarize: Conclude by summarizing the key takeaways from the activity and encourage participants to think about other ways blockchain technology can be applied to improve sustainability, fair trade, and consumer trust in fashion.

Conclusion

The role of the buyer has evolved substantially, and this is due to several reasons. As discussed earlier in this book, there has been a significant change in consumer behaviour and the way people shop. Technological advances have not only changed how we communicate but also how product is made, marketed, and delivered to the consumer. Sustainability is a real concern to the industry, consumers, and the environment, and will impact the future of fashion. Market dynamics have meant that buyers need to be more data-driven, socially responsible and adaptable to a rapidly changing fashion landscape. Developments in e-commerce and online shopping have meant that fashion buyers are adapting their practice to cater for the digital market. Buying decisions are now influenced not only by in-store trends but also by online shopping behaviours, social media trends, and data analytics. Buyers are more conscious of representing a diverse range of styles, sizes, and cultures in their product selections to cater to a broader customer base and working with brands that offer customization options and personalized recommendations to meet individual preferences.

The buyer's role is discussed throughout this book; the role is rigorous but rewarding. Time management is of the upmost importance, as a buyer has to wear many hats at once. Building strong relationships with co-workers within the organization can help to alleviate some of the stress that naturally comes with the job. A buyer's strongest partnership will always be with the merchandiser, the individual who helps to facilitate the planning of merchandise from inception to store deliveries. These two individuals will together create buying and allocation strategies that will enable their brands to maximize their sales through speedy shipment deliveries and re-stocking but, more importantly, that will create brand differentiation for the retailer.

When buyers outsource existing and/or new suppliers and manufacturers, they cultivate external relationships that will also help to strengthen their position, seeking out environmentally friendly and socially responsible suppliers and manufacturers who follow ethical and sustainable practices.

Thanks to various technological advances in communication, logistics, and the development of software tools and platforms like PLM, buyers have the capability to speak directly to globally sourced agencies, preventing risk and range issues from occurring prior to development of the line.

In the latter part of the book, we explored emerging trends in buying and product development and how they influence the buyer, both positively and negatively. These trends, which will eventually become industry norms, are ways for the buyer to further enhance the marketplace, improve resources and become more sustainable while working to gain new customers for what is already a successful brand or retailer. The fast fashion model, categorized by quick production cycles and low prices, is being challenged by the slow fashion movement and buyers now consider the impact of their buying decisions on the environment; we are seeing brands that are increasingly investing in high-quality, timeless pieces over disposable fashion items. Sustainable practice and corporate social responsibility is vital in a quickly expanding global economy. Understanding their organization's initiatives, as well as the initiatives of their stakeholders, will keep the fashion buyer educated as they work towards their profit goals and as their seasonal ranges mature from trend forecast to retail landscape.

We hope that you have enjoyed reading this book and that it helps you on your way to a successful career in fashion buying!

Glossary

AI technology: artificial intelligence technology, computer systems and algorithms that present characteristics of human intelligence.

BCI: Better Cotton Initiative. A global non-profit organization that works to promote sustainable practices in the cotton industry.

Big data: enormous volumes of structured, semi-structured, and unstructured data generated at high speed from numerous sources, such as social media, sensor networks, transaction records, and web applications.

Blockchain: a systematic approach to transparency where all parts of the supply chain are identified (blocks) and joined together in a sequence (chain).

Brand name: a registered name, term, design, symbol, or other feature that easily identifies one seller's product or service from any other.

Brick-and-mortar location: The physical plant at which a retailer or wholesaler will sell their goods or services to consumers.

Co-bot: collaborative robots – a type of industrial robot designed to work alongside humans in a shared workspace.

Consumer connectivity: the capability of consumers to access and connect to several digital services and platforms through different devices, for example smartphones, tablets, laptops, smart TVs, and other internet-enabled devices.

Consumer demographics: those elements that define the organization's customer profile and are defined by ethnicity, income, age, and education. Consumer demographics are quantifiable data that is used typically for marketing purposes.

Corporate social responsibility: a voluntary code created by individual corporations relating to the organization's ethical and environmental stance in its dealings with all of its stakeholders.

Cost price: the price that a buyer will pay for a product or service. This can be with or without shipping depending on where the product is sourced. This is different from the landed price and the target cost price.

Counterfeiting: the deliberate copying of branded merchandise in order to pass it off as the genuine article.

Critical Path (CP): a project management tool that identifies the sequence of tasks or activities that must be completed on time for the purchase order to be completed within the planned schedule.

Data harvesting: also known as data scraping or data mining, refers to the process of collecting large amounts of data from various sources and digital platforms.

Design: the unique look of a fashion product in which design, aesthetics, or natural beauty have been applied to clothing or accessories, differentiating them from any other.

Drop: highly anticipated release or launch of a new collection or product line by a fashion brand, retailer or designer.

E-commerce: refers to an industry that sells goods or services via electronic delivery methods such as the internet or other various electronic networks.

EDI: electronic data interchange. The electronic exchange of business documents, such as purchase orders, invoices, shipping notices between trading partners in a standardized and structured format.

ESG: environmental, social, and governance – a framework to assess the sustainability and ethical impact of companies, organizations, or investments.

E-tailing: the term used to denote a retailer who sells goods or services through electronic methods, specifically the internet. However, this term is loosely used to denote any selling method that is not brick-and-mortar.

GOTS: global organic textile standard – a global certification and labelling system for textiles made from organic fibres.

Key performance indicators (KPIs): different criteria set forth by an organization as a means for measuring performance. KPIs may be based on sales data, consumer market information, etc. to set a standard level of performance practice.

Influencer: an individual with a substantial following and impact on social media platforms by generating and sharing content related to fashion, style, and beauty.

Lead-time: the specific time it takes for a process to be completed, starting from the introduction of the process until its completion.

Licensing: the legalized agreement for another party to manufacture or trade a fashion brand, trademark, design, or patent without fear of legal action.

Line sheet: A visual guide created by the designer, wholesaler, and/or manufacturer, showcasing the available styles for sale that season. Line sheets typically include a fashion flat of the garment, style number, size range, textile options, and delivery dates.

Longevity: a method that emphasizes durability, quality, and ethical production practices, aiming to reduce the negative environmental and social impacts of the fashion industry.

Lookbook: a visual guide created by either the designer, wholesaler, or retailer, showcasing the brand's key looks for the season. Lookbooks typically include a combination of both editorial and catalogue style photography.

Market: a term used to describe a gathering of designers, manufacturers, and/or wholesalers who present their goods for the retail public to purchase from each season.

Merchandising: a term used to represent the promotion of goods sold by retailers and/or the allocation of goods to retailers based on various indicators such as consumer need or fashion trends. One who acts to provide these services on behalf of the retailer is called a merchandiser.

National and international product standards: certain garments and accessories, especially those relating to young children, have to meet stringent national and/or international safety standards; for example, in relation to the flammability of children's nightwear.

National brands: those goods that are produced and distributed by the manufacturer to various retailers, who buy the goods wholesale, redistributing them to their consumers. National brands can be distributed both to national and international markets.

NOOS: never out of stock – a collection of essential, staple, or timeless products, continuously available to be sold and are not subject to seasonal shifts or restricted availability.

OEKO-TEX®: an independent global certification system that tests and certifies textiles and textile products for their safety and sustainability.

Patents: a legally registered novel or non-obvious product, process, or treatment that has intellectual property protection in a/several jurisdiction/s.

PLM: product lifecycle management – a software-driven method used to manage the whole lifecycle of a product, beginning with initial concept and design through manufacturing, distribution, and disposal.

Private label: brands that are produced and distributed by a manufacturer through the manufacturer's own retail outlets. These brands are typically not offered to other retailers.

Qualitative research: a type of research that is collected through the observation of human behaviour and sensory feedback. It is often gathered through the practice of participant observations, non-participant observations, case studies, and ethnographs.

Quantitative research: a type of research that looks at various mathematical models and statistical data that is analysed to determine a hypothesis or theory.

Re-commerce: or reverse commerce is the term used to describe the buying and selling of second-hand or pre-owned goods.

Return to vendor (RTV): a term used in the buying office to denote those goods that have been selected to return to the vendor due to poor quality, slow sales, or any other issues deemed necessary for this action.

SA8000: social accountability – an international standard for social accountability in the workplace.

Social media: platforms and websites that allow users to create and share content, interact with others, and take part in virtual communities.

Stakeholders: those individuals who will be directly affected by the firm's actions or can directly affect the firm or organization in a positive or negative manner.

Stock-keeping unit (SKU): a term used to denote the method by which a retailer provides inventory management for their goods and services. Each item for sale is provided with a unique SKU that provides information such as division, class, origin, season, price, materiality, size, colour, and so on for the retailer to track for inventory purposes.

Supply chain: the set of firms that make and distribute goods and/or services to consumers. This includes manufacturers, suppliers, wholesalers, retailers, and the consumer.

Trade secrets: any competitively sensitive information or a unique way of conducting business that is not openly understood or able to be viewed.

Trademarks: a distinctive, unique, and usually legally registered sign or indicator that helps consumers to realize which organization a fashion product or service emanates from.

Vanity sizing: a term used for retailers who size down from standard market sizing, often creating the illusion that the customer wears a smaller size than they typically would at other retailers.

Visual merchandising: A term used to represent the promotion of goods sold by retailers through the use of display techniques, which include product placement, fixturing, and environmental design (by means of visual design, art, and craft). One who acts to provide these services is called a visual merchandiser.

Industry Resources

Fashion buyers, like all of us, tend to trawl their favourite fashion sites as a leisure activity. However, in a business context, they would tend to use business information services. The better services are subscription-based, although there are also many consumer-focused fashion and styling sites. Whether business or consumer focused, many have differing focuses and information offers – often, they are difficult to easily categorize.

Market shows

While there are various market shows that happen all through the year and around the globe, the following is a list of those markets shows that have been known for bringing innovative and fashion-forward goods to buyers for a variety of product categories.

Capsule Show

A New York-based market show focusing on women's and men's RTW and accessories.

www.capsuleshow.com

COTERIE New York

Collaborating with over 1000 brands and providing a platform for buyers, retailers, experts and influencer's.

www.coteriefashionevents.com

Harrogate Bridal Show

The UK's largest bridal market that caters to the bride/groom, wedding party, and all things related.

www.bridalweek.com

ISPO

International sports trade magazine, events, community, and research agency.

www.ispo.com/en

Pure London

A leading UK fashion buying event

www.purelondon.com

Trend forecasting agencies

Fashion buyers rely a great deal upon their designers and trend forecasting services to help make sense of the deluge of dates, information, and facts available to them. Never in the history of fashion have we been faced with so much information. This is one trend that seems likely to continue.

Doneger Group

A New York-based trend forecasting agency.

www.donegertobe.com

Edelkoort, Inc.

A Dutch-based trend forecasting agency that provides trend books, consulting services, workshops, and seminars.

www.edelkoort.us

Pantone

International colour authority providing a standard in colour language from design to manufacturing. Pantone also provides seasonal colour forecasts to most industries.

www.pantone.com

Promostyl

This France-based agency produces a series of Trendbooks, which are designed to anticipate the current trends in design, fashion, and marketing in order to give their clients a strategic edge in the marketplace. They also provide consulting services on all phases of brand, collection, and product design.

www.promostyl.com

Trendland

A website that contains exciting trend information on both fashion and design.

www.trendland.com

Worth Global Style Network (WGSN)

UK-based trend service delivering what is probably the widest available range of online fashion-business-related services.

www.wgsn.com

Public and subscription services

There are many free fashion blogs and information sites available online. Some of the sites worth checking out are listed here:

Apparel Search

A US-based site about trend forecasting services.

apparelsearch.com/index.htm

Awwwards

Internet design creativity in fashion.

awwwards.com/50-fashion-websites.html

Business of Fashion

Search for fashion news, events style, and jobs.

www.businessoffashion.com

Drapers

Site of UK trade-focused *Drapers* fashion magazine.

www.drapersonline.com

Fashionista

An online fashion news blog.

www.fashionista.com

FJobs

An international site promoting a plethora of fashion jobs around the world as well as industry-breaking news and information.

www.Fashionjobs.com

Just Style.com

Fashion news, events style, and jobs.

www.just-style.com

Style Careers

One of the most respected websites for posting international fashion jobs.

www.stylecareers.com

Talisman Fashion

An international recruiting agency that focuses on the fashion industry.

www.talismanfashion.com

Visual Merchandising/Store Design (VMSD)

A site geared more toward store design and visual merchandising, VMSD also provides industry updates, introduces new technology, and presents various merchandising strategies.

www.vmsd.com

Women's Wear Daily (WWD)

Site of the US trade-focused *Women's Wear Daily* fashion magazine.

www.wwd.com

Index

NOTE: Page references in *italics* refer to captions of photos and figures.

@lilmiquel 151
3D prototyping 158

A
abandoned cart rate 117
actual sales *118*
Adidas 30–3, *30*, *153*
advertising 148–51, *149*, *150*
Africa, manufacturing in 86
American Vogue 37
Americas, manufacturing in 86
Anti-Copying in Design (ACID) 166
Armani, Giorgio 48
artificial intelligence (AI) 148, 150–1, *151*
Asia, manufacturing in 84–5
augmented reality (AR) 153, 157
average customer spend/units per transaction (UPT) *118*
average order value (AOV) 117
Aztec codes 159

B
backward integration 76
Balmain 149, *149*
Bangladesh, manufacturing in 84
Barbie 149, *149*
Berlin Fashion Week 62–5
blockchain technology 158
body scanning 157
bonded fabrics 91
boutiques 6
BOXPARK 154, *155*
brands
　brand names 9
　branding 16, 135–7, 148–51, *149*, *150*, *152*
　product assortment planning 121–2
Brazil, manufacturing in 86
brick-and-mortar locations 7, 48
British Fashion Council (BFC) 41
Browzwear 58
Bulgaria, manufacturing in 85
buyer and designer relationship 70–4
buyer–designer–quality assurance (QA) relationship 70–4, *71*, *72*, *73*
　2D range plan *72*

buyer–merchandiser relationship 114
　see also merchandise planning
buyer–supplier relationship 69–107
　2D range plan *72*
　buyer–designer–quality assurance (QA) relationship 70–4, *71*, *72*, *73*
　case study 99–106, *99*
　developing product categories and selecting lines 88–9
　fabric selection 91–2, *91*, *92*
　fashion lead times and buying cycle, 92–3
　managing supply base 79–80
　meeting with suppliers *80*
　overview 69
　selecting and buying garments 98
　sourcing issues 82–8, *87*
　sourcing suppliers 77–8
　supply chains 74–6, *75*, *94*
　teamwork of 78
　tech packs *73*, 74
　working with representatives 79
buying approaches
　buying cycle 17, 92–3
　fast fashion 17, 22–4
　product-specific purchasing 24–9, *25*, *26*, *27*, *28*, *29*
　theories in fashion buying *18*
　understanding consumer markets, 19–22
buying inspiration *see* marketing
buying markets
　fibre, yarn, and fabric fairs 57–8
　international fashion weeks 58–9
　international ready-to-wear trade fairs 59, *60–1*
　line sheets 53
　lookbooks 53
　overview 51
　purchase orders (POs) 38, *56*
　sales orders 54
　trade exhibitions, fairs, shows 51–7, *54*, *55*, *56*, *57*
　see also marketing
buying teams 12, *13*

183

C

Cala 72
Cambodia, manufacturing in 84
Canada, manufacturing in 86
Carter, Linda 137
Carzana, Paolo *147*
Chanel, Coco 22
charities 16
charity shops 8
cheap clothing, manufacturing of *84*
childrenswear 28, *29*
China, manufacturing in 84
Choi, Sora *149*
CLO Virtual Fashion Incorporated 158, 167–71, *167*
Clo3D 58
colleges, retailing role of 16
colour, product assortment planning 121
colour forecasting 50–1, *52*
communication, efficiency of 89
　see also buyer–supplier relationship
competitive pricing 117
consumer demographics (customer base) *5, 46,* 47, 48–9, 149
　consumer purchasing habits 17
　segmentation of 47
　understanding 17, 19–22
consumer markets 19–24
continuum, of clothing and fashion *5*
conversion rate 117
corporate social responsibility 160–1
　CSR stakeholders 162–4, *163, 164*
　cycle of *160*
　fashion circularity 165
　intellectual property rights (IPR) 166
　vs environmental, social, and governance (ESG) 164, *164*
cost of goods sold 127
customer acquisition cost (CAC) 117
customer lifetime value (CLV) 117
customers
　customer focus 45–7, *49*
　customer profiling 48
　new vs. existing 117
　see also consumer markets; market research
cycles, of buying 17, *18*

D

DALL-E 72
Data Matrix codes 159
decision-making theory 17, *18*
deliveries on time *119*
demographics *5, 46,* 47, 48–9, 147
department stores 4
designer–buyer–quality assurance (QA) relationship 70–4, *71, 72, 73*
　2D range plan *72*
differentiation 47
diffusion of innovation *52*
digital business *158*
digital sales 8–9
directional change, theory of 39
directional fashion change theory *39*
discount customers *49*
discount retail 6
distribution, as retailing role 14–15

E

Eastern Europe, manufacturing in 85–6
eco-friendly technology 157
e-commerce 8–9
　key performance indicators (KPIs) 117
email marketing metrics 117
emotional consumer purchasing motives 19
environmental, social, and governance (ESG) 164, *164*
e-tailing 8–9
ethics 90
Ethiopia, manufacturing in 86
Euromonitor 45
exhibition vendors *56*
expectations, of fashion buyers 11–12
eye-tracking technology 158

F

fabric
　fabric fairs 57–8
　fabric selection 91–2, *92*
　fabric suppliers 15–16
　manufacturing of *91*
　sourcing *93*
　types of 91, *92*
factory outlets/factory village stores 7
fairs 51–7, *54, 55, 56, 57*
fashion buyers/buying 1–36
　approaches 17–24, *18*
　buyer's dilemma *44*
　buying teams and work environment 12–16
　case study 30–3, *30*
　defined 10–11

mantra of *40*
overview 1, *1*
qualifications and expectations 11–12
retail environments and 2–10, *5*, *6*, *7*
skills needed for *14*
working with other retailing roles 13
see also buyer–supplier relationship; buying approaches; marketing; trends in fashion buying
fashion circularity 165
fashion cycles *24*
Fashion Group International 40
fashion shows
    international fashion weeks 58–9, *60–1*
    overview 51–7, *54*, *55*, *56*, *57*
Fashion United 41
fast fashion 17, 22–4
female garment types 25–6, *26*
fibre fairs 57–8
fibre types 91
final range preparation 134
Financial Times (UK) 43
FOMO (fear of missing out) strategy 150
forecasting sales and stock 124–5
Forever 21, 8
forward integration 76
France, manufacturing in 85

G

garment technologists 13–14
garments, selecting and buying 98
Gerber Technology 90
Germany, manufacturing in 85
Girlfriend Collective 165
global marketing, impact of *150*
global organic textile standard (GOTS) 164
global sourcing 83–7, *87*
GreenStride™ *37*
grey market 6
gross margin *118*

H

H&M *28*, 148, 165
Harrop, Mark 138–43, *140*
Harvey Nichols *5*
hierarchy of needs 17, *18*
hierarchy of product types 25
home goods 28, *29*
Hungary, manufacturing in 85
hypermarkets 7

I

import merchandising 114
impulse customers *49*
India, manufacturing in 84
Indonesia, manufacturing in 85
Industry, The 41
initial season buying plan 123–5, *123*
    forecasting sale and stock 124–5
    merchandise assortments 124
    range planning 122–4, *123*
inspiration *see* marketing
intellectual property rights (IPR) 166
International Foundation of Fashion Technology Institutes (IFFTI) 41
international marketing
    case study 62–5, *63*
    international market reports 45
Italy, manufacturing in 85

J

just in time (JIT) *see* fast fashion

K

Kate Spade *6*
key performance indicators (KPIs) 111, 114, 117, *118*, *119*
Kim, Simon J.H. 167–71, *167*, 168
knitted fabrics 91
Kotler's 1967 theory of analysis, planning and control 122

L

last year (LY) sales 116
"Le Chouchou", Jacquemus's Fashion Show 23/24 *110*
lead times 92–3, *93*, 96–8, *97*
Levi's *152*, 165
lifestyle accessories 28, *29*
line sheets 53
lines, selecting 88–9
lookbooks 53
loyal customers *49*

M

magic mirrors 157
Maison Margiela 149, *149*
male garment types 27–8, *28*
managing, of samples 136
mantra *40*
manufacturing, sourcing issues 82–3, *83*, *87*
markdowns *116*, 117, *119*, 127–9

market intelligence 38–9, *38, 39*
market levels *6*
market research
    consumer segmentation 47
    for customer base 45, *46*
    customer focus 45–7, *49*
    customer profiling 48
    demographics *5*, 45, *46*, 47, 48–9, 147
    formal 43
    international market reports 45
    overview 42–4
    quantitative market trends 47
marketing 37–66
    buyers and market intelligence 38–9, *38, 39*
    case study 62–5
    directional fashion change theory *39*
    industry insight and 40–1
    market research 42–4, *43, 44*
    marketing mix 42, *43*
    overview 37, *37*
    promotional activities 148–9, *149, 150, 152, 153, 155*
    as retailing role 16
    trend forecasting 49–51, *50, 51, 52*
markup 125
Maslow, Abraham 17, *18*
McKinsey & Company 45
McQueen, Alexander 23, 69
media 16, 154–5
    see also social media
meetings
    merchandise planning *120*
    with suppliers *80*
menswear *see* male garment types
merchandise assortments 124
merchandise planning 111–45
    buyer's instinct vs planning 114–15
    buyer–merchandiser relationship 114
    case study 138–43, *139, 140*
    collection examples *110, 133, 135*
    defined 112
    initial season buying plan 122–5, *123*
    merchandise pricing 125–9
    overview 111
    process of 120–2, *120*
    product lifecycle *128*
    product sampling and final range preparation 134–7
    risk and range 129–31, *130*
    success of 115–19
    visual merchandising 152, *153*

merchandise pricing 125–9
merchandisers, defined 38
Mexico, manufacturing in 86
Middle East, manufacturing in 86
Mintel 45
mobile commerce 158–60
motivation 19

N

national brands 9–10, *10*, 134
National Retail Federation (NRF) 41
need-based customers *49*
net achieved margin after discount (NAMAD) *119*
net sales 127
never out of stock (NOOS) products 112
new vs. existing customers 117
Nigeria, manufacturing in 86

O

Oculus 157
online pure players 8–9
'open to buy' (OTB) 121, 127
Outform TM 153
    QR code 153

P

Park, Stephen 99–106, *99*
Patagonia 165
patronage, consumer purchasing motives 19
Peclers 50
performance of suppliers, monitoring 80–2
Peru, manufacturing in 86
planned sales *118*
planning, as retailing role 14–15
Poland, manufacturing in 85
pop-up shops 154, *155*
positioning 47
Prada, Miuccia 116
press 16, 154–6
price point 127
pricing 125–9, *126*
printed fabrics 92
private labels 9–10, *10*, 134, 136
product affinity 117
product categories, developing 88–9
product complexity *113*
product lifecycle *128*
product lifecycle management (PLM) software systems 138–43, *139, 140*
product lines, selecting 89–90
product sampling 134–6

product-specific purchasing 24–9, *25*, *26*, *27*, *28*, *29*
profiling, customer 48
promotional activities
    artificial intelligence (AI) 151–2
    branding, advertising, marketing 148–9, *149*, *150*, *152*
    public relations (PR) 16, 155–6
    showtelling and pop-up shops 154, *155*
    social media 150–1
    visual merchandising 152, *153*
    see also marketing
promotional samples 136
psychographics 47
public relations (PR) 16, 155–6
purchase orders (POs) 38, *56*

Q

QR codes 159–60, *159*
qualifications, for fashion buyers 11–12
qualitative performance criteria, for suppliers 82
quantitative market trends 47
quantitative performance criteria, for suppliers 81

R

range planning 122–4, *123*
    complete new product category 124
    core product revision 124
    line extensions 124
    new product lines 124
    reposition 124
range width and depth, balancing 131
rational consumer purchasing motives 19
Reebok 149, *149*
representatives, of suppliers 79
research *see* market research
Retail Design Institute (RDI) 41
retail environment
    buyer's relationship with 2–3
    continuum of clothing and fashion *5*
    future of *3*
    market levels *6*
    national brands vs. private labels 9, *10*
    overview 2
    retail staff 3
    types of retail stores 4–10
Retail Management Advisors 137
retail merchandising 114
retail price, setting 125

retailing roles
    colleges and universities 16
    fabric suppliers 15–16
    garment technologists 13–14
    marketing and branding 16
    planning and distribution 14–15
    press and media 16
    teamwork and 12, *13*
    trade bodies/associations, and charities 16
return rate 117
returns *119*
risk and range size issues 129–32, *130*
Rodgers, Everette *52*
Romania, manufacturing in 85

S

sales margin (SM) *118*
samples
    product sampling and final range preparation 134–7
    providing for press 156
sealing, of samples 136
Searson, Andrew 30–3, *30*
seasonality *113*
SEEK 62–5
segmentation 47
showtelling 154, *155*
size
    product assortment planning 121
    risk and range size issues 129–32, *130*
skills, needed by fashion buyers *14*
slow fashion 22–4, *24*
smartphones 158–60
social media
    metrics 117
    promotional activities 148–9
sources of inspiration *see* marketing
sourcing issues 82–7, *83*, *84*, *87*
sourcing trips 92–3
Sousa, Miquela 151
South Africa, manufacturing in 86
Spain, manufacturing in 85
specialty retailers 4
Sri Lanka, manufacturing in 85
stakeholders 162–4, *164*
standards 14
stock level *118*
stock turn/weeks cover (ST/WC) *118*
stock-keeping units (SKUs) 12
stores, retail 4–10
Stumbaugh, Stephanie 99–106, *99*

Style 3D Fashion 3.0 58
style tribes *21*
supermarkets 7
supplier relationships *119*
suppliers
    managing supply base 79–80
    meeting with *80*
    performance monitoring 80–2
    sourcing 77–8
    teamwork between buyers and 78
    working with representatives of 79
    see also buyer–supplier relationship
supply chains 74–6, *75*, *94*
    buyer's role in 74–6
sustainable technology 157
Swatchbook 58

T
target audiences 47
teamwork 12, *13*, 78
tech packs *73*, 74
technology 156–61
    changing *97*, 157–58
    digital business *158*
    improved business practice 156–7
    mobile commerce 158–9
    QR codes 159–60, *159*
    smartphones 158–60
    web data codes 158–60
textile, product assortment planning 122
thrift shops 8
Timberland *37*
TOMS *163*
trade bodies/associations 16
trade exhibitions 51–7, *54*, *55*, *56*, *57*
trend forecasting *119*
    concepts, colors, sources 50–1, *52*
    diffusion of innovation *52*
trends in fashion buying 147–75
    case study 169–73, *169*, *170*
    corporate social responsibility 160–1, *160*, *163*, *164*
    overview 147, *147*
    promotional activities 148–60, *149*, *150*, *152*, *153*, *155*
    technology 156–60, *158*, *159*

trickle-across effect 39
trickle-down theory 39
trickle-up theory 39
Turkey, manufacturing in 85–6

U
Ukraine, manufacturing in 85
United Kingdom, manufacturing in 85
universities, retailing role of 16
unpredictability *113*
Urban Outfitters 5

V
VEJA 164, *164*
vendors *54*, *56*
Verdict 45
vertical integration 76
Vietnam, manufacturing in 84
vintage shops 8
virtual reality (VR) 157
visual merchandising 114, 152, *153*
VisualHound 72
Vizoo 58
VMSD 40

W
Wall Street Journal (US) 43
Wang, Victoria 168
web data codes 158–60
website traffic 117
Western Europe, manufacturing in 85
WhichPLM 138–43, *139*, *140*
Winpenny, Damien 62–5, *63*
womenswear *see* female garment types
World Intellectual Property Organization 166
Worth Global Style Network (WGSN) 104, 180
woven fabrics 91

X
XRite 58

Y
yarn fairs 57–8

Acknowledgements and Picture Credits

With special thanks:

From Clare
I would like to express my gratitude to my friends and family for their enduring support during the research and writing stages, with a special mention to my partner Martyn Catlow. I extend my appreciation to everyone who played a role in bringing this book to life, with a special acknowledgement to Gayle Fenny and Nathalie Evans. Additionally, I'd like to thank my colleagues, students, and friends at the Manchester Fashion Institute at Manchester Metropolitan University for their support in this venture.

From Dimitri
Many thanks to my friends and family who have put up with me during the research and writing process and whom I actively ignored during this time. Thank you to David Shaw and the Bloomsbury team for allowing me to be a part of this project. A very teary-eyed thank you to Colette Meacher, of whom I have grown so fond during our time working together. I can't imagine doing this without you, and I really appreciate your continual support, encouragement, and uncanny ability to deal with my large personality.

Picture credits:
All reasonable attempts have been made to trace, clear, and credit the copyright holders of the images reproduced in this book. However, if any credits have been inadvertently omitted, the publisher will endeavour to incorporate amendments in future editions.

0.1 Jim Heimann Collection/Contributor
0.2 Photo by Jeff Spicer/BFC/Getty Images for BFC
0.3 Colin Hawkins
1.1 Photo by Arturo Holmes/Getty Images
1.2 Francesco Carta fotografo
1.3 Photo by Joe Maher/Getty Images for Harvey Nichols
1.4 Photo by Belinda Jiao/SOPA Images/LightRocket via Getty Images
1.6 Photo by Michael M. Santiago/Getty Images
1.7 Photo by BRYAN R. SMITH/AFP via Getty Images
1.8 Photo Illustration by Pavlo Gonchar/SOPA Images/LightRocket via Getty Images
1.9 Photo by Clemens Bilan/Getty Images
1.10 Photo by Mark Kerrison/In Pictures via Getty Images
1.11 Photo by Michael Brochstein/SOPA Images/LightRocket via Getty Images
1.12 Photo by John Keeble/Getty Images
1.13 Photo by John Keeble/Getty Images
1.14 Photo by John Keeble/Getty Images
1.15 Capuski
1.16 Hispanolistic
1.21 Photo by Matthew Sperzel/Getty Images
1.22 Photo by Matthew Sperzel/Getty Images
1.23 Photo by Matthew Sperzel/Getty Images
1.24 Photo by Matthew Sperzel/Getty Images
1.25 Photo by Matthew Sperzel/Getty Images
1.27 Photo by Edward Berthelot/Getty Images
1.28 Photo by Edward Berthelot/Getty Images
1.29 Photo by Edward Berthelot/Getty Images
1.30 Edward Berthelot / Contributor
1.31 Photo by Kirstin Sinclair/FilmMagic
1.32 Photo by Brian Dowling/Getty Images
1.33 Photo by Edward Berthelot/Getty Images
1.34 Photo by Jeremy Moeller/Getty Images
1.35 Philip Openshaw
1.36 Photo By Eduardo Parra/Europa Press via Getty Images
1.37 Photo by Al Zeta/Getty Images
1.38 Photo by Gonzalo Marroquin/Patrick McMullan via Getty Images
1.39 Andrew Searson
2.1 Photo by Dimitrios Kambouris/Getty Images for Timberland

2.2 Photo by Dimitrios Kambouris/Getty Images for Timberland
2.7 Photo by Edward Berthelot/Getty Images
2.8 Photo by Edward Berthelot/Getty Images
2.9 Eva-Katalin
2.11 Photo by Vittorio Zunino Celotto/Getty Images; Photo by Jeremy Moeller/Getty Images; Photo by Edward Berthelot/Getty Images
2.12 Photo by Kurita Kaku/Gamma-Rapho via Getty Images
2.14 Photo by George Chinsee/WWD/Penske Media via Getty Images
2.16 Photo by Fatih Erel/Anadolu Agency/Getty Images
2.17 Photo by Adam Berry/Getty Images for IMG
2.18 CFOTO/Future Publishing via Getty Images
2.19 Photo by Howard Schnapp/Newsday RM via Getty Images
2.20 Photo by: Edwin Remsberg/VW PICS/UIG via Getty Images
2.22 Photo by Tristar Media/Getty Images
2.23 Damien Winpenny
3.1 Photo by David M. Benett/Dave Benett/Getty Images for Alexander McQueen
3.2 Mint Images
3.3 Chelsea Lauren/Stringer
3.4 Gayle Fenny
3.5 Gayle Fenny
3.7 Photo by Cole Burston/AFP; Photo by Howard Schnapp/Newsday RM via Getty Images
3.11 Photo by Fairchild Archive/WWD/Penske Media via Getty Images
3.14 Photo by andresr via Getty Images
3.15 Aleksandar Georgiev
3.16 Leon Harris
3.17 Photo by Wang Gang/China News Service/VCG via Getty Images
3.18 Photo by Jean-Philippe Ksiazek/AFP via Getty Images
3.19 Dougal Waters
3.21 VictorHuang

3.23 Photo by Wang Gang/China News Service via Getty Images
3.24 Photo by Wang Gang/China News Service via Getty Images
3.25 Stephen Park
3.26 Stephanie Stumbaugh
4.1 Photo by Pierre Suu/WireImage
4.2 Photo by Stephane Cardinale – Corbis/Corbis via Getty Images
4.3 Photo by Stephane Cardinale – Corbis/Corbis via Getty Images
4.4 Photo by Justin Tallis/AFP
4.5 Photo by Mario Tama/Getty Images
4.10 Huizeng Hu; John Lawson; Peter Dazeley
4.11 victorhe2002; clu; fotostorm; Phamai Techaphan
4.16 Photo by Christopher Polk/Billboard via Getty Images
4.17 Photo by Matt Jelonek/WireImage
4.18 Photo by Giovanni Giannoni/WWD via Getty Images
4.19 hudiemm; PATRICIA DE MELO MOREIRA/AFP; Christophe Pallot/Agence Zoom/Getty Images
4.20 Mark Harrop
5.1 Photo by Jeff Spicer/BFC/Getty Images
5.2 Photo by Melodie Jeng/Getty Images
5.3 Photo by Marc Piasecki/Getty Images
5.4 Grady Coppell
5.5 Photo by M. Caulfield/WireImage for PMK/HBH
5.6 Photo by VCG/VCG via Getty Images
5.7 Photo by Mike Kemp/In Pictures via Getty Images
5.8 Photo by Vittorio Zunino Celotto/Getty Images
5.9 Photo by Edward Berthelot/Getty Images
5.10 Photo by Aldara Zarraoa/Getty Images
5.12 Photo by John M. Heller/Getty Images
5.13 Photo by John M. Heller/Getty Images
5.14 Photo by Edward Berthelot/Getty Images
5.15 CLO Virtual Fashion
5.16 CLO Virtual Fashion
5.17 CLO Virtual Fashion